W9-BNA-574

BISCUITS BREADS & COOKIES

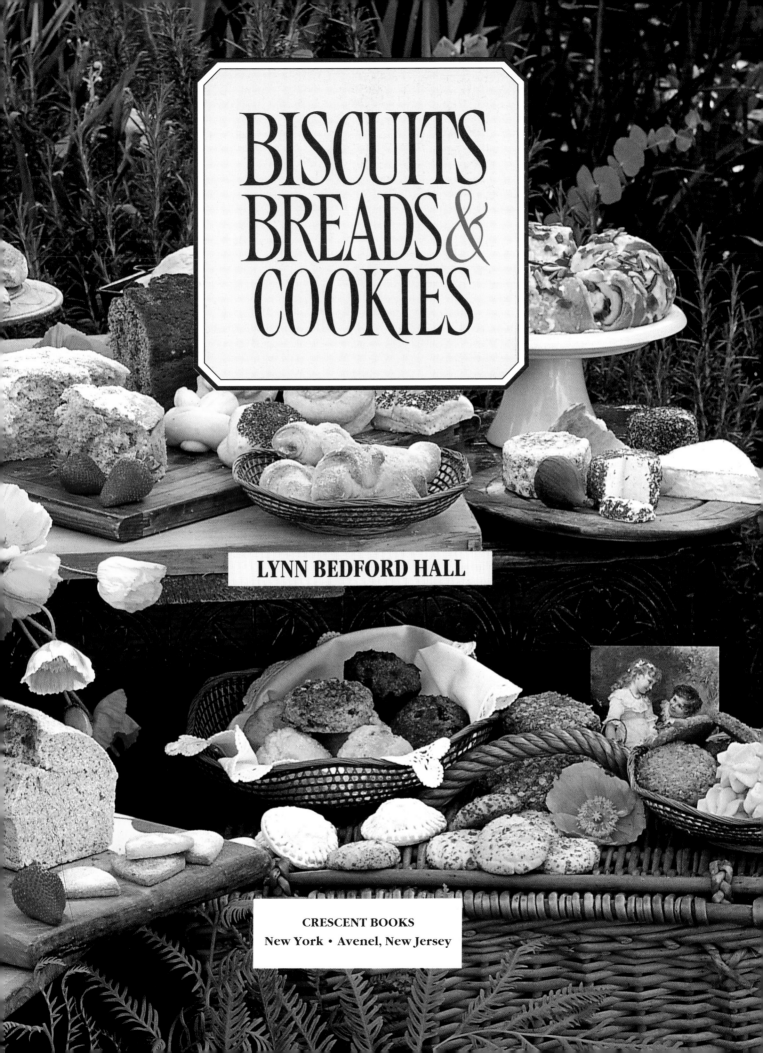

BISCUITS BREADS & COOKIES

LYNN BEDFORD HALL

CRESCENT BOOKS
New York • Avenel, New Jersey

This 1994 edition published by Crescent Books, distributed by Outlet
Book Company, Inc., a Random House Company,
40 Engelhard Avenue, Avenel, New Jersey 07001

Random House
New York • Toronto • London • Sydney • Auckland

Copyright © 1993 in text Lynn Bedford Hall
Copyright © 1993 in photographs and illustrations New Holland
(Publishers) Ltd
Copyright © 1993 New Holland (Publishers) Ltd

All rights reserved. No part of this publication may be
reproduced, stored in a retrieval system, or transmitted, in any
form or by any means, electronic, mechanical, photocopying
recording or otherwise, without the prior written permission of
the copyright owners and publishers.

ISBN 0 517 10347 8

Editors: Elizé Lübbe, Alison Leach
Designer: Petal Palmer
Illustrator: Tobie Beele
Photographs: Anthony Johnson
Styling: Vo Pollard

Typesetting by Bellset
Reproduction by Unifoto
Printed and bound in Singapore by Tien Wah Press (Pte.) Ltd

CONTENTS

FOREWORD
7

COOKIES & BARS
8

YEAST BREADS
36

HEALTH BREADS
42

ROLLS
48

QUICK BREADS
54

MUFFINS
64

BISCUITS
70

HOME-BAKING AT ITS BEST
74

INDEX
78

FOREWORD

This book is the result of a very long baking affair. For months I have mixed and kneaded, creamed and rolled, risen and cut, and it has left me – not only a little floury – but also convinced that home-baking should definitely be put back on the culinary map.

There are, however, so many good cookies, biscuits and breads available these days, that many people have lost the urge to make their own. This is a pity, because not only is baking both relaxing and enjoyable, but nothing out of a package can match the nose-twitching aroma of freshly baked bread, biscuits and muffins.

Bread-baking, in particular, can become an addictive pastime. Kneading is wonderfully therapeutic and gets rid of a lot of aggression on the days when you're feeling uptight.

Baking cookies, quick breads, biscuits and muffins can be equally satisfying and is a means to endless creativity. For example, in certain recipes I have substituted whole-wheat flour for some of the more-traditional cake flour. This does mean that the end product will be a little heavier and different in texture from the refined versions, but rather more wholesome and in line with the present swing to less processed ingredients. You will also notice that I have cut down a little on sugar and salt, proving that one can jiggle recipes to adapt to your own tastes and convictions, and I am sure you will find yourself adding many personal touches to my ideas.

I have, without exception, used extra-large eggs, and I suggest you do the same, or else you might end up with too little liquid and, therefore, a different result. For creaming and mixing most cookies and sweet loaves, I have used a hand-held Philips three-speed electric mixer. I cannot guarantee the same results if you try creaming with a wooden spoon. Using an electric mixer is quick, easy and thorough. However, I rarely use the dough hooks for bread, simply because I think it is important to develop a personal relationship with your dough. If you feel and knead it with your hands it becomes, in today's idiom, user-friendly, and you will soon learn to tell when the right consistency has been reached.

I hope, with this book, to help define the trend back to home baking. Even if it is only on special, less pressurized days, home cooks all over are definitely displaying a predilection for presenting their families with bakes that didn't start out pre-wrapped in a shopping cart. I've done it, and so can you, and while test-baking for this book there were many occasions on which I called my family to come and peer in through the glass oven door to watch whatever it was rising, spreading and browning. Which proves that baking can become a communal experience and when the results are good, the reward is a companionable sharing.

And finally, all that is left to be said is to wish you the best of baking, and happy munching!

Lynn Bedford Hall

COOKIES & BARS

SPICE COOKIES

My grandma used mutton fat, rather than butter, and left her dough to stand overnight, followed by a long session of rolling and cutting out little circles with a glass. She had lots of time, and would doubtless have disapproved of these easy spice 'n' slice cookies, using everyday ingredients, but do try them – they're so delicious.

1¼ cups all-purpose flour or white bread flour
1¼ cups whole-wheat bread flour
1 teaspoon baking powder
pinch of salt
½ teaspoon baking soda
1 teaspoon apple pie spice
1 teaspoon ground cinnamon
¼ teaspoon ground cloves
½ teaspoon ground ginger
½ cup butter, softened
½ cup sugar
½ cup soft light brown sugar
1 egg
2 tablespoons sweet sherry

Sift both flours with baking powder, salt, baking soda and spices. Return any bran left in the sifter. Cream butter, then slowly add both sugars, beating well. Beat egg with sherry and beat into butter mixture with 1 teaspoon of the flour mixture to make a soft dough.

Shape dough into two 1¼-inch diameter sausage shapes. Wrap in waxed paper and chill for about 1 hour. Using a sharp knife, slice into ¼-inch thick circles and place on greased baking sheets, leaving room for spreading. Bake at 325°F for 15 minutes, then transfer to wire racks to cool and crisp.
Makes about 70

Bright and dainty little Coconut-Cherry Stars (page 19) and deliciously crisp Lemon Sesame Snaps.

NUT AND OATMEAL COOKIES

1 cup plus 2 tablespoons butter, softened
1 cup sugar
few drops vanilla extract
1 egg, beaten
2 cups all-purpose flour
3 tablespoons cornstarch
pinch of salt
2 teaspoons baking powder
1 cup oatmeal
1 cup finely chopped pecans

Cream butter, sugar and vanilla. Add egg and mix well. Sift flour, cornstarch, salt and baking powder and add. Mix until combined, then add oatmeal and nuts. Knead with your hands until mixture forms a ball. Pinch off small pieces, roll into balls, and place on greased baking sheets. Press down lightly with a fork and bake at 350°F on middle shelf of oven for 20 minutes. Cool on wire racks.
Makes about 48

BROWNIES

There are hundreds of versions of this family favorite: this one is like a light, thinly crusted chocolate cake.

3 eggs
¾ cup sugar
3 tablespoons soft light brown sugar
3½ ounces semisweet chocolate, broken up
½ cup butter
1¼ cups all-purpose flour
1 teaspoon baking powder
pinch of salt
1 cup chopped walnuts or pecans
few drops vanilla extract

Beat the eggs and sugars together until thick and pale. Melt the chocolate and butter together over very low heat. Beat the chocolate into the egg mixture. Sift the flour, baking powder and salt together, then add to egg mixture and stir until combined. Stir in nuts and vanilla.

Pour into a greased 10- × 8-inch baking pan. Bake at 350°F for 35 minutes until just firm and starting to crack around the edges. Be careful not to overbake. Cut into squares and leave to cool in pan. These brownies keep well.
Makes about 36

HINT
● *Keep cookies crisp by storing them in airtight containers with a sprinkling of sugar between the layers.*

LEMON SESAME SNAPS

Deliciously crisp, brown cookies. Toasting brings out the flavor of sesame seeds – spread them out on a large baking sheet and place in oven, either preheated, or when you turn it on prior to baking. Remove when golden brown, watching carefully because they burn easily.

½ cup butter, softened
few drops vanilla extract
6⅓ tablespoons sugar
2 teaspoons finely grated lemon peel
5 teaspoons honey
½ cup white bread flour
pinch of salt
½ teaspoon baking soda
½ cup whole-wheat flour
½ cup sesame seeds, toasted

Cream the butter, vanilla, sugar, lemon peel and honey together. Sift white bread flour, salt and baking soda together. Mix into the creamed mixture, then add whole-wheat flour and sesame seeds. Combine well to a soft dough.

Shape into a ball, pinch off small pieces, roll into balls and place on greased baking sheets, leaving room for spreading. Press down with tines of a fork, making a crisscross pattern. Bake at 350°F for 12 minutes. Leave on baking sheet for 1 minute to crisp, then transfer to wire racks to cool.
Makes about 30

BASIC BUTTER COOKIES

Make several batches and flavor the cookies in a variety of ways – these are very quick to mix with the help of a hand-held electric mixer.

½ cup butter, softened
¾ cup sugar
1 egg, lightly beaten
few drops vanilla extract
2 cups white bread flour
1 teaspoon cream of tartar
½ teaspoon baking soda

Cream butter and sugar until light, then add egg and vanilla and beat. Sift dry ingredients and add. Mix to a soft dough and then shape into a ball with your hands. Pinch off walnut-size pieces and place on greased or nonstick baking sheets, leaving room for spreading. Press down lightly with the tines of a fork. Bake on the middle shelf of the oven at 350°F for 12 minutes, or until pale beige. Cool on wire racks.
Makes about 30

VARIATIONS
Coffee-Pecan Butter Cookies
Substitute soft light brown sugar for the white sugar. Beat egg lightly with 1 tablespoon instant coffee granules and the vanilla extract, until coffee has dissolved. Add ⅓ cup finely chopped pecans to the dough and top each with a pecan piece.

Lemon-Peel Butter Cookies
Cream butter and sugar with 1 teaspoon finely grated lemon peel. Use only 1 cup white bread flour when sifting, then add 1 cup whole-wheat flour and ⅓ cup finely chopped mixed peel. Top each cookie with a golden raisin.

Chocolate Butter Cookies
Sift 2 teaspoons cocoa powder with the dry ingredients and add 1½ ounces grated semisweet chocolate to the dough. Press a chocolate morsel into the top of each cookie.

MUNCHIES

Knobbly, wholesome cookies.

½ cup self-rising flour
1 teaspoon ground cinnamon
1 cup whole-wheat flour
¾ cup sugar
⅔ cup vegetable oil
2 eggs
1 cup oatmeal
1 cup mixed dried fruit
½ cup shredded coconut

Sift self-rising flour and cinnamon, then mix in whole-wheat flour. Beat together sugar, oil and eggs. Add to dry ingredients together with oatmeal, fruit and coconut. Mix very well to a soft dough. Push large teaspoonfuls off onto greased baking sheets. Bake at 350°F for 18 minutes. Using a spatula, transfer to wire racks to cool and crisp.
Makes about 40

COCONUT-LEMON CRISPIES

Pale golden, crunchy little cookies.

7 tablespoons vegetable oil
¾ cup sugar
1½ teaspoons finely grated lemon peel
1 egg
2 cups white bread flour
½ teaspoon baking powder
pinch of salt
1 cup shredded coconut
extra sugar

Place oil, sugar and lemon peel in a deep rather than a wide mixing bowl, and beat very well. Add egg and beat

NOTE
● *Butter cookies should always be baked on the middle shelf of the oven to avoid browned bottoms, therefore it is best to bake them in relays.*

until mixture is creamy and yellow. Sift together flour, baking powder and salt, add to creamed mixture and mix well, then beat in coconut. Roll into balls and press flat between your palms. Dip tops in extra sugar and place on greased baking sheets, sugar sides up, leaving room for spreading. Bake at 350°F for 15 minutes until just browning around the edges. Cool on wire racks.
Makes about 30

COOKIE-PRESS COOKIES

This dough keeps its shape well and may be used to make any design, but is particularly attractive made into daisy shapes with a cookie press, with half a candied cherry pressed into the center. Alternatively, sprinkle with cinnamon-flavored sugar [mix ½ teaspoon ground cinnamon with 1 teaspoon sugar], or top with finely chopped almonds, pressed in lightly. The dough may also be flavored with grated lemon or orange peel, or the cookies may be sandwiched together using vanilla butter frosting.

½ cup butter, softened
½ cup sugar
1 egg
few drops vanilla extract
1¾ cups all-purpose flour
3 tablespoons cornstarch
pinch of salt

Cream butter and sugar. Beat the egg and vanilla together and add. Mix well, then add flour sifted with cornstarch and salt. Combine well to make a soft dough and then press into a ball, rather like shortbread. Fill the cookie press and press out onto lightly greased baking sheets, not too close, because although the mixture does not contain any raising agent, the cookies spread slightly as the butter melts. Bake at 400°F for 12 to 15 minutes until pale beige in color. Cool on wire racks.
Makes 30 to 36

FROM THE BACK: *Chocolate Cookies; Coconut-Lemon Crispies; Date Knobs; Cookie-Press Cookies.*

CHOCOLATE COOKIES

There are many versions of this favorite cookie. Chocolate morsels usually retain their shape, while chopped chocolate melts in the baking.

½ cup butter, softened
4 tablespoons soft light brown sugar
4 tablespoons sugar
1 egg
few drops vanilla extract
½ teaspoon baking soda
2 teaspoons hot water
1½ cups all-purpose flour
pinch of salt
2 teaspoons cocoa powder
3½ ounces semisweet chocolate
½ cup chopped walnuts or pecans

Cream butter and both sugars until light. Beat egg with vanilla and add, mixing well. Stir in baking soda dissolved in hot water. Sift in flour, salt and cocoa. Combine well. Chop chocolate in food processor and add together with nuts, mixing to a soft dough. Then either pinch off small balls and flatten between your palms before placing on greased baking sheets, or push off rough mounds from tip of teaspoon. Bake at 350°F for 20 minutes. Cool on wire racks.
Makes about 36

DATE KNOBS

Crisp little cakes, stuffed with dates.

PASTRY
2 cups all-purpose flour
3 tablespoons cornstarch
3 tablespoons confectioners' sugar
¾ cup butter, chilled
1 egg
few drops vanilla extract
extra confectioners' sugar

FILLING
1½ cups chopped pitted dates
1 teaspoon lemon juice
3 tablespoons water
¼ cup chopped walnuts

Gently heat dates, lemon juice and water until dates can be mashed with a wooden spoon. Add nuts and leave to cool.

Sift dry ingredients. Cut in butter. Beat egg and vanilla and add. Mix well. Knead into a ball – do not add any liquid. Roll out thinly on a floured board and cut into 2- to 3-inch circles. Reroll trimmings until all the dough has been used. Place a heaped spoon of filling in the center of each circle, cover with a second circle and seal edges with a fork. Prick each top twice. Place on a greased baking sheet. Bake at 350°F for 18 to 20 minutes or until pale gold. Remove to a wire rack and dredge with sifted confectioners' sugar.
Makes about 14

Coconut-Currant Snaps

A typical cookie-jar cookie, that is economical and easy.

½ cup butter, softened
¾ cup sugar
1 egg
few drops vanilla extract
2 cups self-rising flour
pinch of salt
1 cup shredded coconut
½ cup currants
extra sugar

Cream butter and sugar. Mix in egg beaten with vanilla. Sift flour with salt and add to creamed mixture together with coconut. Finally mix in currants. Knead to a ball, then pinch off small pieces and roll into balls. Press flat between your palms, dip tops in extra sugar and place on greased baking sheets, leaving room for spreading. Bake at 350°F for 15 minutes until just beginning to brown. Cool on wire racks.
Makes about 50

Melting Moments

½ cup butter, softened
½ cup sugar
1 egg, lightly beaten
few drops vanilla extract
1½ cups self-rising flour
pinch of salt
1 cup coarsely crushed bran flakes, or
1½ cups crushed corn flakes

Cream butter and sugar. Add egg and vanilla and beat well. Sift flour with salt and add. Mix thoroughly to form a soft ball, then pinch off small pieces. Roll into balls and roll in crushed cereal. Arrange on greased baking sheets, leaving room for spreading, and press down lightly with a fork. Bake on middle shelf of oven (as they brown quickly on the bottom) at 350°F for 15 minutes. Cool on wire racks.
Makes about 30

Carrot and Coconut Jumbles

Big, chewy and wholesome.

½ cup butter, softened
1 cup soft light brown sugar
1 cup whole-wheat flour
1 cup all-purpose flour
1 cup shredded coconut
1 cup oatmeal
1½ cups coarsely grated carrots
1 teaspoon baking soda
pinch of salt
2 teaspoons ground cinnamon
½ teaspoon grated nutmeg
½ cup golden raisins or
seedless raisins
2 eggs, lightly beaten
few drops vanilla extract
½ cup vegetable oil

Cream butter and sugar. Add flours, coconut, oatmeal, carrots, baking soda, salt, spices and golden raisins or seedless raisins. Beat together eggs, vanilla and oil. Add to creamed mixture and mix very well – use an electric mixer – mixture will eventually form a soft dough. Push heaped teaspoonfuls off onto lightly greased baking sheets, leaving room for spreading, and press down lightly with a fork. Bake at 350°F for 20 minutes. Let stand for 1 minute to crisp, then use a spatula to remove to wire racks to cool.
Makes about 48

Whole-wheat, Honey and Coconut Crisps

Caramel-colored, crunchy cookies.

½ cup butter, melted
5 teaspoons honey
6 tablespoons soft light brown sugar
1 cup whole-wheat flour
pinch of salt
½ teaspoon baking soda
2 teaspoons hot water
½ cup shredded coconut
few drops vanilla extract

Mix melted butter with honey, sugar, flour and salt. Add baking soda dissolved in hot water. Mix in coconut and vanilla. Combine thoroughly until mixture forms a soft ball. Pinch off small pieces and roll into balls. Place on ungreased baking sheets, leaving room for spreading. Bake at 350°F for 12 to 14 minutes until a rich brown color. Cool on wire racks.
Makes about 28

Florentines

A thin, lacy cookie with dried fruit and nuts, coated with chocolate.

¼ cup butter, softened
4 tablespoons sugar
5 teaspoons all-purpose flour, sifted
⅓ cup chopped almonds
12 candied cherries, chopped
3 tablespoons chopped golden raisins
2 knobs preserved ginger in syrup,
chopped
3 tablespoons chopped mixed peel
3½ ounces semisweet chocolate

Cream butter and sugar well. Fold in flour. Add almonds and fruit. Spoon large teaspoonfuls, far apart, onto baking sheets, preferably nonstick but otherwise greased and dusted with cornstarch. Flatten lightly with the back of a spoon. Bake at 350°F for about 10 minutes or until browned with lacy edges. Remove from oven and, using a spoon, push lightly into neat circles. Using a spatula, transfer carefully to a wire rack to cool.

Melt chocolate very gently over simmering water – do not let it get too hot – and spread evenly over flat side of each cooled cookie. Run a fork through the chocolate as it hardens to make the characteristic wavy pattern. When cool and set, store in airtight container.
Makes about 14

COCONUT-ALMOND CRISPS

Big, crunchy cookies.

½ cup butter, softened
¾ cup sugar
few drops vanilla extract
1 egg, lightly beaten
2 cups self-rising flour
pinch of salt
¾ cup shredded coconut
⅓ cup finely chopped toasted almonds

Cream butter, sugar and vanilla until light. Add egg and beat. Sift in flour and salt and mix well. Add coconut and almonds and knead to a soft ball. Pinch off small pieces, roll into balls and place on greased baking sheets, leaving plenty of room for spreading. Press twice with the tines of a fork, making a crisscross pattern. Bake at 350°F for 20 minutes or until a deep beige color. Cool on wire racks.
Makes about 40

VANILLA CONDENSED MILK DROPS

1 cup plus 2 tablespoons butter,
softened
6 tablespoons sugar
7-ounce can condensed milk
3 cups all-purpose flour
2 teaspoons baking powder
pinch of salt
few drops vanilla extract

Cream butter and sugar. Beat in condensed milk. Sift flour, baking powder and salt and add to creamed mixture. Finally add vanilla, then mix to a soft dough. Push small mounds off tip of teaspoon onto greased or nonstick baking sheets. Flatten with the tines of a fork, in a crisscross pattern. Sprinkle lightly with cinnamon-flavored sugar, if desired. Bake at 350°F for 15 minutes or until just beginning to brown. Cool on a wire rack.
Makes about 54

FROM THE BACK: *Carrot and Coconut Jumbles; Melting Moments; Whole-wheat, Honey and Coconut Crisps.*

ONE-BOWL RAISIN AND BRAN BARS

1 cup self-rising flour
¾ cup sugar
1 cup shredded coconut
¾ cup raisins
3 tablespoons chopped mixed peel
5 tablespoons sunflower seeds
¼ cup soft butter, diced
7 tablespoons vegetable oil
1 egg, beaten
1⅓ cups bran flakes
few drops vanilla extract

Put ingredients into large bowl in order listed. Using an electric mixer, beat until thoroughly combined. Spread evenly into a lightly greased 9-inch square baking pan. Bake on middle shelf of oven at 350°F for about 30 minutes until firm and well browned. Cut into bars and cool in pan.
Makes about 18 large bars.

SOUR CREAM-SPICE COOKIES

1 cup plus 2 tablespoons butter, softened
1 teaspoon ground cinnamon
1 teaspoon apple pie spice
¼ teaspoon grated nutmeg
2 cups soft light brown sugar
1 egg, lightly beaten
½ cup sour cream
4 cups all-purpose flour
½ teaspoon baking soda
¼ teaspoon salt

Cream butter with spices. Slowly beat in sugar. Beat in egg and sour cream. Sift flour with baking soda and salt. Add to creamed mixture and combine to a soft dough. Shape into a ball with your hands. Pinch off small pieces and roll into balls, flouring hands when necessary. Place on greased baking sheets and press down with fork, making a crisscross pattern. Bake on middle shelf of oven at 350°F for 15 minutes. Cool on wire racks.
Makes about 72

FROM THE TOP: *Spiced Golden Raisin Slices; Bran Flake Crisps; Coconut Slices.*

WHEAT GERM AND MUESLI CRISPS

¼ cup soft butter, diced
¼ cup vegetable oil
1 egg
few drops vanilla extract
1 cup self-rising flour
¾ cup sugar
¼ teaspoon salt
2 tablespoons untoasted wheat germ
⅓ cup shredded coconut
½ cup seedless raisins or golden raisins
¾ cup muesli (Swiss-style cereal)

Put ingredients into bowl in order listed. Use an electric mixer to beat until butter has dissolved and mixture can be kneaded into a ball. Pinch off pieces slightly larger than a walnut, arrange on greased baking sheets and press down with the tines of a fork. Bake on middle shelf of oven at 350°F for about 20 minutes until lightly browned. Use a spatula to transfer to wire racks to cool and crisp.
Makes about 30 large cookies

BRAN FLAKE CRISPS

½ cup butter, softened
1 cup sugar
1 cup white bread flour
1 teaspoon baking powder
pinch of salt
½ teaspoon baking soda
1 teaspoon apple pie spice
1 egg
few drops vanilla extract
1⅓ cups bran flakes
1 cup shredded coconut
1 cup oatmeal

Cream butter and sugar until light. Sift flour, baking powder, salt, baking soda and apple pie spice and add. Mix well, then add egg beaten with vanilla. When combined, stir in coarsely crushed bran flakes, coconut and oatmeal. Roll into small balls and place on greased baking sheets, leaving plenty of room for spreading. Press down with bottom of a glass. Bake at 350°F for 20 minutes until browned. Cool on wire racks.
Makes about 40

SPICED PECAN CRISPS

½ cup butter, softened
1 cup soft light brown sugar
1 egg
few drops vanilla extract
2 cups plus 2 tablespoons all-purpose flour
½ teaspoon baking powder
¼ teaspoon baking soda
1 teaspoon ground cinnamon
½ teaspoon grated nutmeg
½ cup chopped pecans

Cream butter and sugar until fluffy. Beat in egg and vanilla. Sift dry ingredients and add to creamed mixture, combining thoroughly. Lastly stir in pecans. Form into sausages, wrap in waxed paper and freeze for about 45 minutes, until firm.

To bake, slice fairly thinly and place on a lightly greased baking sheet. Bake at 350°F for 12 to 15 minutes, until pale golden brown. Cool on wire racks.
Makes about 54

SPICED GOLDEN RAISIN SLICES

Made without either egg yolks or butter, these are baked in flat strips and then cut into diagonal slices.

1 egg white
1 teaspoon lemon juice
½ cup sugar
7 tablespoons light corn syrup
½ cup vegetable oil
3 cups all-purpose flour
1 teaspoon baking soda
pinch of salt
1 teaspoon ground ginger
1 teaspoon apple pie spice
½ teaspoon grated nutmeg
1 cup golden raisins

Beat the egg white, lemon juice, sugar, syrup and oil thoroughly. Sift the flour, baking soda, salt and spices together, then add slowly to the first mixture, beating. Stir in golden raisins and mix to a dough. Roll the dough into four 1-inch thick sausage shapes. Place on greased baking sheets and flatten lightly. Bake on the middle shelf of the oven at 350°F for 18 minutes, or until nicely browned. Cool for a few minutes and then cut diagonally into slices about ¾ inch thick. Cool on wire racks.
Makes about 40

EASTER BISCUITS

These biscuits are ideal for lunch boxes because they do not crumble.

2 cups all-purpose flour
pinch of salt
1 teaspoon baking powder
1 teaspoon apple pie spice
½ teaspoon ground cinnamon
¼ teaspoon grated nutmeg
½ cup butter, softened
½ cup sugar
⅓ cup currants
4 tablespoons chopped mixed peel
1 egg, lightly beaten
extra sugar

Sift flour, salt, baking powder and spices. Cut in butter. Stir in sugar, currants and peel. Add egg. Mix to a dough and then shape into a ball. Do not add any liquid, just knead lightly until mixture holds together. Pat out on floured board and then roll gently with a rolling pin to flatten to about ½ inch thick. Cut out circles with a fluted 2½-inch cutter. Place on greased baking sheets. Bake at 350°F for 12 to 15 minutes until lightly browned. Remove to a wire rack, sprinkle with sugar. Leave to cool.
Makes 30 to 40

COCONUT SLICES

Once chilled, this dough is sliced into cookies in seconds, making refrigerator cookies the quickest and easiest to prepare for the oven.

10 tablespoons butter, softened
1 cup sugar
1 egg
few drops vanilla extract
2 cups all-purpose flour (half whole-wheat bread flour may be used)
pinch of salt
½ teaspoon baking soda
1 cup shredded coconut

Cream butter and sugar until light. Add egg and vanilla and beat well. Sift flour with salt and baking soda and mix into creamed mixture. Add coconut. Work into a ball and then divide into two 1¼-inch thick sausage shapes. Wrap in waxed paper and chill for 1 hour.

Using a sharp knife, cut into ¼-inch slices and place fairly far apart on ungreased baking sheets. Bake at 325°F on middle shelf of oven for about 12 minutes. Cool on a wire rack.
Makes about 60

MOCHA-CHOCOLATE LOGS

Dipped into melted chocolate and rolled in nuts, these are attractive little cookies with the texture of shortbread.

4 teaspoons instant coffee granules
4 teaspoons water
1 cup plus 2 tablespoons butter, softened
½ cup sugar
few drops vanilla extract
2½ cups all-purpose flour
½ cup cornstarch
pinch of salt
semisweet chocolate and finely chopped almonds

Dissolve coffee granules in water. Add to butter and sugar and cream until light. Add vanilla. Sift flour, cornstarch and salt, then add to creamed mixture and beat to a soft dough – a hand-held electric mixer may be used. Using a pastry bag with a star-shaped nozzle, pipe 2-inch long logs onto ungreased baking sheets. Bake at 325°F for 15 to 20 minutes until a pale golden brown. Leave on baking sheets for a few minutes before transferring to wire racks to cool.

Melt the chocolate in a small pan over hot water. Dip one end of each into the melted chocolate and then roll in nuts until coated. Return to the wire racks for the chocolate to set.
Makes about 48

CINNAMON-JAM COOKIES

Quick to make and economical.

½ cup butter, softened
¾ cup soft light brown sugar
1 egg, lightly beaten
1 cup white bread flour
1 teaspoon baking soda
pinch of salt
2 teaspoons ground cinnamon
3 tablespoons smooth apricot jam
1 cup whole-wheat flour

Cream butter and sugar. Add egg and beat well. Sift white bread flour, baking soda, salt and cinnamon and add to creamed mixture together with the jam. Mix well and then add whole-wheat flour and combine to make a soft dough. Push little mounds off the tip of a teaspoon onto greased baking sheets, leaving room for spreading. Bake at 350°F for 10 minutes or until lightly browned. Cool on wire racks. Store in airtight container, with a sprinkling of sugar between the layers.
Makes about 40

SNICKERDOODLES

1 cup plus 2 tablespoons butter, softened
1 cup sugar
2 eggs, lightly beaten
few drops vanilla extract
3 cups white bread flour
5 tablespoons cornstarch
2 teaspoons cream of tartar
1 teaspoon baking soda
pinch of salt
3 tablespoons sugar
2 teaspoons ground cinnamon
½ teaspoon apple pie spice

Cream butter and sugar. Add eggs and vanilla and beat until creamy. Sift flour, cornstarch, cream of tartar, baking soda and salt. Add to creamed mixture and mix to a soft dough. Pinch off walnut-size pieces and roll into small balls. On a large plate, mix sugar with spices. Roll each ball in this mixture, coating well, then place well apart on ungreased baking sheets. Sprinkle any leftover sugar mixture over the tops, and press down lightly with back of fork. Bake at 350°F for 15 minutes. Initially they will rise like top hats and then settle into disk shapes. Cool on wire racks.
Makes about 48

GRANNY'S GINGERSNAPS

2½ cups all-purpose flour
1 cup sugar
½ teaspoon baking soda
½ teaspoon apple pie spice
pinch of salt
2 teaspoons ground ginger
½ cup butter, softened
1 egg
5 teaspoons thin honey
slivers of preserved ginger in syrup

Sift dry ingredients together. Cut in butter. Beat in egg and honey and mix into dough, then knead into a ball. Do not add any liquid. Pinch off walnut-size pieces of dough and roll into balls. Place on nonstick or greased baking sheets, with room to spread. Press a sliver of preserved ginger into each. Bake at 325°F for 20 minutes or until lightly browned. Cool on wire racks and store in airtight container.
Makes 30 to 36

FRUITY REFRIGERATOR SQUARES

1 cup plus 2 tablespoons butter, softened
4 cups confectioners' sugar
2 eggs, beaten
2½ cups coarsely broken vanilla wafers
1 cup shredded coconut
few drops vanilla extract
⅓ cup chopped mixed peel
⅓ cup golden raisins

Melt butter over low heat. Slowly blend in sifted confectioners' sugar. Keeping heat very low, stir in eggs – on no account should the mixture boil or eggs will scramble. Add crumbs. Mix well, remove from the heat and add remaining ingredients. Combine thoroughly, using a wooden spoon. Press flat into a shallow dish greased with soft margarine. Cool, and then chill before cutting into small squares. Store in the refrigerator, wrapped in plastic wrap.
Makes about 48

FROM THE TOP: *Mocha-Chocolate Logs; Cinnamon-Jam Cookies; Fruity Refrigerator Squares; Granny's Gingersnaps.*

OLD-FASHIONED JAM SQUARES

A cookie base spread with jam and a crumble topping – this recipe fills a large baking pan and is easily made using an electric mixer.

1 cup plus 2 tablespoons butter, softened
1 cup sugar
2 eggs
few drops vanilla extract
4 cups all-purpose flour
1 tablespoon baking powder
generous pinch of salt
smooth apricot jam
confectioners' sugar

Cream butter and sugar well. Beat eggs with vanilla, then add and mix well. Sift flour, baking powder and salt, then beat into creamed mixture and mix well until mixture forms a soft ball that holds together. Pinch off two-thirds of dough and press and pat out evenly into lightly greased 15-×10-inch baking pan. Spread generously with jam. Using the coarse side of a grater, grate remaining dough over the top – don't press down, simply spread with a fork. (There is no need to chill the dough first. It should not stick if you run the grater under cold water now and then.) Bake on middle shelf of oven at 350°F for about 35 minutes until golden brown. Cut into squares and leave to cool in pan. Sift a little confectioners' sugar over the squares before removing.
Makes about 32

BROWN SUGAR COOKIES

Crisp, buttery cookies like Grandma used to make to fill the cookie jar.

1 cup plus 2 tablespoons butter, softened
1 cup soft light brown sugar
1 egg, lightly beaten
few drops vanilla extract
3 cups self-rising flour
pinch of salt
quartered pecans or candied cherries (optional)

Old-fashioned Jam Squares; Coconut Macaroons; Coconut-Cherry Stars; Almond Crescents, studded with cloves.

Using an electric mixer, cream butter and sugar until light. Add egg and vanilla and beat. Add flour and salt and continue beating until very well combined, then shape into a smooth ball. Pinch off small pieces and roll into balls the size of a large marble. Place on ungreased baking sheets and press down with a fork in a crisscross pattern. If using, gently press a quartered pecan or cherry into the top of each. Bake at 350°F for 15 minutes. Transfer to wire racks to cool.
Makes about 48

ALMOND CRESCENTS

These kourabiedes are the national cookies of Greece, served at weddings, birthday celebrations and christenings. Because they are similar to shortbread in texture, they should be handled delicately.

1 cup plus 2 tablespoons butter, softened, preferably unsalted
½ cup sugar
1 egg yolk
1 tablespoon brandy
3 cups all-purpose flour
5½ tablespoons cornstarch
½ cup finely chopped toasted almonds
whole cloves
sifted confectioners' sugar

Cream butter and sugar until pale and fluffy. Add yolk beaten with brandy and beat until combined. Sift flour with cornstarch and beat in gradually. Add almonds and knead until smooth. Pinch off small pieces and shape into crescents. Place on ungreased baking sheets and insert a clove into the top of each. Bake at 300°F for about 30 minutes. Test by cutting one in half – there should not be any trace of a buttery streak. While still warm, carefully roll the crescents in confectioners' sugar. Place on wire racks and sift more confectioners' sugar over the crescents – they should be well coated. Leave before storing in airtight container.
Makes about 48

COCONUT-CHERRY STARS

Bright, dainty little cookies.

½ cup butter, very soft
3 tablespoons confectioners' sugar, sifted
1 scant cup all-purpose flour
5 teaspoons cornstarch
few drops vanilla extract
5 tablespoons shredded coconut
12 candied cherries, halved
5 teaspoons water (optional)

Cream butter and confectioners' sugar. Sift flour and cornstarch, add to creamed mixture and beat well. Add vanilla and coconut. Mix well, adding up to 5 teaspoons water if dough is too stiff. Using a pastry bag fitted with a star-shaped nozzle, pipe onto ungreased baking sheets. Press half a cherry into each. Bake at 325°F for 20 minutes until pale golden. Cool on a wire rack.
Makes 16 to 24

> NOTE
> ● *It is important to use soft butter, extra-large eggs, and an electric mixer for the next recipe, otherwise the mixture will not bind sufficiently.*

SPICED COFFEE DROPS

Disk-shaped, soft and spicy.

1 cup plus 2 tablespoons butter, softened
2 cups soft light brown sugar
2 extra-large eggs
1 tablespoon instant coffee granules
½ cup cold water
4 cups white bread flour plus 2 teaspoons extra
1 teaspoon baking soda
¼ teaspoon salt
1 teaspoon ground cinnamon
½ teaspoon grated nutmeg
large pinch of ground cloves
semisweet chocolate morsels (optional)

Cream butter and sugar. Beat in eggs, one at a time. Dissolve coffee in water and add together with the 2 teaspoons flour. Beat well. Sift flour, baking soda, salt and spices. Mix into creamed mixture to make a soft dough. Chill for at least 1 hour. Using a teaspoon, push mounds of dough off onto greased baking sheets, leaving plenty of room for spreading. Press a chocolate morsel lightly into the top of each, or leave plain. Bake at 350°F for 13 to 15 minutes, until golden brown. Using a spatula, transfer to wire racks to cool. Store in airtight container, with a sprinkling of sugar between layers.
Makes about 80

MUESLI BARS

½ cup butter, softened
1 cup soft light brown sugar
1 egg, beaten
1 cup whole-wheat flour
½ cup oatmeal
¾ cup muesli (Swiss-style breakfast cereal)
2 tablespoons shredded coconut
½ cup golden raisins
1 teaspoon baking powder
1 teaspoon ground cinnamon
½ teaspoon apple pie spice
½ cup chopped nuts, or 5 tablespoons sunflower seeds

Cream butter and sugar. Add egg and beat well. Add rest of ingredients and mix to a soft dough – use an electric mixer. The mixture will seem rather crumbly, but it binds together as you press it out. Press into a lightly greased 13- × 8-inch jelly roll pan. Bake at 350°F for 20 minutes. Cut into bars – they will be very soft, but will crisp up while cooling. Cool in pan, then carefully transfer to a wire rack and leave until completely cool.
Makes about 24

COCONUT MACAROONS

1 egg
½ cup sugar
few drops vanilla extract
pinch of salt
1¾ cups shredded coconut
quartered candied cherries, or halved almonds

Beat egg, sugar, vanilla and salt until very light and creamy. Gradually beat in coconut to make a moist and crumbly mixture. Using a teaspoon, push small mounds onto a greased baking sheet which has been dusted with cornstarch. Pinch with fingers into pyramids. Top the macaroons with cherries or almonds. Bake at 300°F for 20 minutes or until just beginning to brown. Gently loosen with spatula and transfer to a wire rack to cool.
Makes about 20

CHOCOLATE CRINKLES

The ultimate crunchy sandwiched cookies, filled with melted chocolate.

½ cup butter, softened
½ cup sugar
½ cup self-rising flour
pinch of salt
½ cup whole-wheat flour
⅔ cup shredded coconut
few drops vanilla extract
5 teaspoons cocoa powder
2 tablespoons boiling water
melted semisweet or milk chocolate

Cream butter and sugar. Add self-rising flour sifted with salt. When well mixed add whole-wheat flour, coconut and vanilla. Mix well, then stir in cocoa creamed with boiling water. Beat into flour mixture to make a soft dough. Gather into a ball and pinch off small pieces the size of large marbles. Place on greased baking sheets. Press down heavily with fork to score deeply. Bake at 350°F for 15 minutes. Cool on a wire rack. When cool, sandwich together with melted chocolate.
Makes about 22 cookie sandwiches

RAISIN-OATMEAL BARS

¼ cup butter, softened
4 tablespoons soft light brown sugar
3 tablespoons light corn syrup
2 eggs, lightly beaten
½ cup all-purpose flour
1½ teaspoons baking powder
1 teaspoon apple pie spice
½ cup whole-wheat flour
1 cup seedless raisins
½ cup oatmeal
confectioners' sugar (optional)

Cream butter and sugar. Add syrup and eggs and beat well. Sift all-purpose flour, baking powder and spice and mix into creamed mixture. Stir in whole-wheat flour, raisins and oatmeal. Combine well – the mixture will be soft and sticky. Turn into a greased 9-inch square baking pan and spread evenly, using a dampened spoon or a rubber spatula. Bake at 350°F for 25 minutes, until browned, risen and firm. Cut into bars and cool in pan. Leave plain, or, before removing, sift a little confectioners' sugar on top.
Makes about 18 large bars

FRUITY OATMEAL CRISPS

½ cup butter, softened
½ cup soft light brown sugar
few drops vanilla extract
½ cup all-purpose flour
1¾ cups oatmeal
⅔ cup mixed dried fruit
pinch of salt
½ teaspoon baking soda
2 teaspoons hot water

Cream butter, sugar and vanilla. Add flour, oatmeal, fruit and salt. Mix well, then beat in baking soda dissolved in hot water. Mix to a soft dough, pinch off small pieces and roll into balls, flouring your palms occasionally if necessary. Place on greased baking sheets and press down lightly with a fork. Bake at 350°F for 15 minutes before transferring to wire racks to cool.
Makes about 28

PEANUT BUTTER COOKIES

3 tablespoons peanut butter
½ cup butter, softened
few drops vanilla extract
¾ cup soft light brown sugar
1 egg, lightly beaten
1 cup white bread flour plus
1 teaspoon extra
pinch of salt
½ teaspoon baking soda
1 cup whole-wheat bread flour

Cream peanut butter, butter and vanilla. Beat in sugar very well or it will not dissolve. Add egg plus 1 teaspoon extra flour and beat well. Sift in white bread flour, salt and baking soda. Finally mix in whole-wheat bread flour and knead until dough holds together. Roll small pieces into balls and place on greased baking sheets, leaving room for spreading. Flatten with a wet fork in a criss-cross pattern. Bake at 350°F for 20 minutes. Cool on wire racks
Makes about 36

Crisp Chocolate Crinkles and elegant Vanilla Viennese Twirls.

SPICED COCONUT COOKIES

A simple, crunchy cookie with spices adding a lovely zip to the flavor.

½ cup butter, softened
¾ cup sugar
1 egg
few drops vanilla extract
2 cups self-rising flour
pinch of salt
1 teaspoon ground cinnamon
¼ teaspoon grated nutmeg
¾ cup shredded coconut
pecans, halved (optional)

Cream butter and sugar until light. Beat egg with vanilla, then add, mixing well. Sift flour, salt and spices and add, then finally mix in coconut and combine thoroughly. Knead into a ball with your hands, then pinch off small pieces and roll into balls. Place on greased baking sheets, allowing for spreading. Press flat with a fork, or press half a pecan into the top of each. Bake at 350°F for 15 to 18 minutes until a deep beige color. Cool on wire racks.
Makes about 36

CRUNCHIES

A super version of a family favorite; it is designed to fill a 15- × 10-inch jelly-roll pan to the brim, requires slightly less butter and sugar than usual, and is made extra nutritious with the addition of raisins and/or sunflower seeds.

3 cups oatmeal
1½ cups soft light brown sugar
1 cup whole-wheat bread flour
½ cup all-purpose flour
1 cup shredded coconut
⅔ cup seedless raisins
⅓ cup sunflower seeds
1 cup plus 2 tablespoons butter
3 tablespoons honey
2 teaspoons baking soda

Mix oatmeal, sugar, flours, coconut, raisins and sunflower seeds. Melt butter and honey together over low heat – the mixture will brown slowly and this adds to the flavor. Stir in baking soda and when mixture froths, add to dry ingredients. Mix well and press firmly into a greased 15- × 10-inch jelly-roll pan. Bake on middle shelf of oven at 350°F for 18 to 20 minutes until richly browned. Cut into jumbo bars and remove when cool.
Makes about 30 jumbo bars

VANILLA VIENNESE TWIRLS

Melt-in-the-mouth little shortbreads, sandwiched with vanilla butter frosting.

1 cup plus 2 tablespoons butter, softened
⅓ cup confectioners' sugar, sifted
2 cups all-purpose flour
3 tablespoons cornstarch
few drops vanilla extract

FROSTING
½ cup confectioners' sugar, sifted
2 tablespoons butter, softened
few drops vanilla extract

Cream butter and sugar. Sift flour and cornstarch. Add to creamed mixture together with vanilla and mix well to a soft dough. Spoon the mixture into a pastry bag. Pipe rosettes onto ungreased baking sheets. Bake at 325°F for 20 minutes until pale golden. Cool on a wire rack.

Beat ingredients for frosting together until smooth. Use to sandwich cookies.
Makes about 24 single cookies

CHOCOLATE LOGS

1 cup plus 2 tablespoons butter, softened
½ cup confectioners' sugar, sifted
few drops vanilla extract
1 tablespoon cocoa powder
1¾ cups all-purpose flour
5½ tablespoons cornstarch
pinch of salt

VANILLA BUTTER FROSTING
½ cup confectioners' sugar, sifted
nut-sized piece of soft butter
few drops vanilla extract
1 teaspoon milk
chocolate sprinkles

Cream butter, confectioners' sugar and vanilla until light. Sift cocoa, flour, cornstarch and salt and add to creamed mixture. Mix to a soft dough. Fill a pastry bag fitted with a fluted nozzle. Pipe into 3-inch long logs onto ungreased baking sheets. Bake at 325°F for 30 minutes, then cool on a wire rack.

To make frosting, combine all ingredients, except sprinkles, until creamy. Spread over tops of logs and decorate with chocolate sprinkles.
Makes about 36

CHOCOLATE CHIP COOKIES

Large, crisp cookies studded with nuts and chocolate morsels, which do not melt during baking.

½ cup butter, softened
⅓ cup sugar
4 tablespoons soft light brown sugar
1 egg
few drops vanilla extract
1¼ cups all-purpose flour
3 tablespoons cornstarch
½ teaspoon baking soda
pinch of salt
½ cup chopped walnuts or pecans
1 cup semisweet chocolate morsels

Cream butter with both sugars. Beat egg with vanilla and add, mixing well. Sift flour, cornstarch, baking soda and salt together. Add to creamed mixture, mixing to a soft dough. Stir in nuts and chocolate morsels. Shape dough into a ball, pinch off pieces and roll into balls, flouring your palms occasionally if necessary. Place on greased baking sheets, leaving room for spreading, and flatten lightly with a fork. Bake at 350°F for 15 minutes. Carefully transfer to wire racks to cool.
Makes about 40

FRUIT-OATMEAL SQUARES

These cookies keep well and are similar to Crunchies (page 21).

1½ cups mixed dried fruit
1 cup plus 2 tablespoons butter
2 tablespoons honey
2¾ cups oatmeal
1 cup whole-wheat flour
1 cup white bread flour
2 tablespoons wheat germ
1 cup shredded coconut
¾ cup soft light brown sugar
2 teaspoons apple pie spice
2 teaspoons baking soda

Put fruit, butter and honey into heavy-bottomed saucepan and bring to a slow boil, stirring to melt the butter.

Mix oatmeal, flours, wheat germ, coconut, sugar and spice in large bowl. Add baking soda to hot mixture, stirring vigorously, and when mixture froths, stir into dry ingredients. Mix well and then press into a greased 15- × 10-inch jelly-roll pan. Pat in firmly and evenly.

Bake on middle shelf of oven at 350°F for 15 to 20 minutes until browned. Cut into squares and leave in pan until cool. Store in an airtight container.
Makes about 35

LEMON-GOLDEN RAISIN SNAPS

These super cookies spread into very crisp, golden-brown rounds. Store them in an airtight container for up to a week.

½ cup butter, softened
few drops vanilla extract
finely grated peel of 1 lemon
½ cup sugar
½ cup all-purpose flour
pinch of salt
½ teaspoon baking soda
½ cup whole-wheat flour
½ cup golden raisins or seedless raisins

Cream butter with vanilla, lemon peel and sugar until light. Sift all-purpose flour with salt and baking soda. Add to creamed mixture and mix.

Add whole-wheat flour and when combined, add golden raisins. Mix well, then knead into a ball. Pinch off small pieces, roll into balls, and place on greased baking sheets, leaving room for spreading. Flatten two ways, making a crisscross pattern, with a fork dipped into water.

Bake at 350°F for 15 minutes. Let stand for 1 minute to crisp, then use a spatula to transfer to a wire rack to cool.
Makes about 28

WHOLE-WHEAT-AND-OATMEAL GINGER CRISPS

1 cup plus 2 tablespoons butter, softened
1 cup soft light brown sugar
1 cup whole-wheat flour
2½ cups oatmeal
1 tablespoon ground ginger
¼ teaspoon salt
few drops vanilla extract
½ teaspoon baking soda
3 tablespoons boiling water

Cream butter and sugar until light. Add flour, oatmeal, ginger, salt and vanilla. Mix well. Add baking soda dissolved in boiling water. Combine thoroughly, then work into a soft ball. Place teaspoonfuls of dough on greased baking sheets, leaving room for spreading. Bake at 350°F for about 15 minutes until lightly browned and spread into flat circles. Leave on baking sheets for a minute to crisp, then transfer with spatula to wire racks to cool.
Makes about 48

ORANGE COOKIE-PRESS COOKIES

Delicately flavored, with a short texture. Serve plain, or sandwich with orange-flavored butter frosting.

½ cup butter, softened
3 tablespoons sugar
finely grated peel of ½ orange
1 cup all-purpose flour
3 tablespoons cornstarch
½ cup shredded coconut

Cream butter, sugar and peel until very light. Mix in flour sifted with cornstarch. Add coconut and then beat well until mixture forms a ball. Using a cookie press, press into desired shapes onto ungreased baking sheets. Bake at 325°F for 20 minutes. Cool on a wire rack.
Makes about 24

FROM THE TOP: *Fruit-Oatmeal Squares; Lemon-Golden Raisin Snaps; Orange Cookie-Press Cookies; Chocolate Chip Cookies.*

SIMPLE COCOA CRISPS

½ cup soft light brown sugar
½ cup sugar
½ cup vegetable oil
1 egg, beaten
½ cup shredded coconut
few drops vanilla extract
pinch of salt
½ teaspoon baking soda
½ cup whole-wheat bread flour
2 cups oatmeal
5 teaspoons cocoa powder

Put ingredients into bowl in above order and beat until well mixed – the dough will be crumbly. Press together into a ball with your hands, then scoop up teaspoonfuls and place on greased baking sheets, leaving plenty of room for spreading. Pinch into little pyramids with your fingers. Bake at 350°F for 20 minutes. Leave on baking sheets to crisp for 1 minute before transferring with spatula to a wire rack to cool.
Makes about 28

OATMEAL, GOLDEN RAISIN AND COCONUT BARS

¼ cup butter
¼ cup vegetable oil
1 cup oatmeal
½ cup golden raisins
1 cup self-rising flour
½ cup sugar
½ cup shredded coconut
few drops vanilla extract

Place butter and oil in a small heavy-bottomed saucepan and heat gently just until butter melts. Mix remaining ingredients and stir in melted shortening. Using an electric mixer, beat to a soft, crumbly consistency. Press firmly into a greased 9-inch square baking pan. Bake on middle shelf of oven at 350°F for 25 minutes, until just beginning to color. Cut into bars and leave in pan until cool.
Makes about 18

Simple Cocoa Crisps; Orange Liqueur Wafers; Quick Date-and-Nut Bars.

WALNUT CRISPS

Delicious, crisp cookies.

2 cups all-purpose flour
1 teaspoon baking powder
pinch of salt
½ teaspoon baking soda
1 teaspoon apple pie spice
½ cup butter
½ cup soft light brown sugar
½ cup sugar
1 egg
few drops vanilla extract
½ cup finely chopped walnuts

Sift the flour, baking powder, salt, baking soda and spice together. Cream the butter and slowly add the brown and white sugars, beating well. Beat the egg and vanilla together and add to butter mixture, then mix in the flour mixture – an electric mixer is perfect for the job. Lastly add walnuts. Form the dough into two long sausage shapes, wrap in waxed paper and chill until firm enough to slice. Cut into thin slices. Bake on ungreased baking sheets at 350°F for about 15 minutes. Cool on wire racks. Store in an airtight container.
Makes about 54

Carrot, Date and Sunflower Seed Cookies

Big, flat, quick-mix cookies.

½ cup soft light brown sugar
½ cup sugar
½ cup butter, softened
1 egg, beaten
¾ cup coarsely grated carrots
1 teaspoon ground cinnamon
¼ teaspoon grated nutmeg
pinch of salt
½ teaspoon baking soda
½ cup whole-wheat bread flour
3 cups oatmeal
⅔ cup finely chopped pitted dates
½ cup sunflower seeds, preferably toasted

Beat all the ingredients, except sunflower seeds, until very well combined. Add sunflower seeds and mix to a soft dough. Scoop up teaspoonfuls and push onto greased baking sheets, leaving plenty of room for spreading. Bake at 350°F for 15 minutes, then allow to crisp on baking sheets for about 1 minute before carefully transferring, with a spatula, to wire racks to cool.
Makes about 40

Chinese Chews

These soft bars firm up with storing and develop a gingery flavor.

½ cup butter, softened
¾ cup soft light brown sugar
2 eggs
1 cup white bread flour
1 teaspoon baking powder
½ cup chopped walnuts or pecans
⅔ cup chopped pitted dates
⅓ cup chopped candied cherries
2 large knobs preserved ginger in syrup, chopped
few drops vanilla extract
sugar

Cream butter and sugar. Add eggs, one by one, beating well. Sift flour and baking powder, then add nuts and fruit and toss to mix. Stir into creamed mixture. Add vanilla and mix well to a thick batter. Turn into a greased 10- × 8-inch baking pan, spreading evenly. Bake at 350°F for 25 minutes or until light brown and firm. Dust with a little sugar, cut into bars and leave in pan until cold.
Makes about 24

Orange Liqueur Wafers

Light, melt-in-the-mouth little slices, to serve with sorbets or ice cream.

½ cup butter, softened
½ cup sugar
5 teaspoons orange-flavored liqueur
1 cup all-purpose flour
3 tablespoons cornstarch
pinch of salt
1 teaspoon finely grated orange peel
extra sugar

Cream butter, sugar and liqueur until fluffy. Sift flour, cornstarch and salt and blend into butter mixture. Mix in orange peel, then shape into a ball and roll into a long, smooth sausage shape. Wrap in waxed paper and chill for about 1 hour.

Using a sharp knife, slice dough thinly. Arrange on an ungreased baking sheet, leaving room for spreading. Bake at 350°F for 10 minutes, or until pale golden. Dust with sugar and leave to cool slightly on baking sheet, then lift carefully onto wire racks to cool completely.
Makes 42 to 48

Quick Date-and-Nut Bars

1½ cups chopped pitted dates
2 eggs, lightly beaten
⅓ cup soft light brown sugar
¼ cup vegetable oil
½ cup whole-wheat flour
½ cup oatmeal
1 teaspoon baking powder
1 teaspoon apple pie spice
pinch of salt
½ cup chopped walnuts or pecans
few drops vanilla extract
confectioners' sugar

Mix all ingredients, except confectioners' sugar, in the order given. Spoon evenly into a greased 9-inch square baking pan. Bake at 350°F for 25 minutes, until brown and firm. Cut into bars and cool in pan. Dust with confectioners' sugar when cold.
Makes about 18 large bars

Muesli Munchies

½ cup all-purpose flour
1 teaspoon cream of tartar
½ teaspoon baking soda
pinch of salt
1 teaspoon apple pie spice
1 cup whole-wheat flour
¾ cup soft light brown sugar
⅔ cup vegetable oil
2 eggs
½ cup muesli (Swiss-style breakfast cereal)
½ cup golden raisins
½ cup shredded coconut

Sift dry ingredients. Add whole-wheat flour. Beat together sugar, oil and eggs. Add to dry ingredients together with muesli, golden raisins and coconut. Mix very well to a soft dough. Push large teaspoonfuls off onto greased baking sheets, with plenty of room to spread. Flatten lightly with tines of a fork dipped into water. Bake at 350°F for 18 minutes. Using a spatula, transfer to wire racks to cool.
Makes about 30

SUNFLOWER SEED AND HONEY COOKIES

1 cup oatmeal
1 cup white bread flour
½ cup sugar
½ cup shredded coconut
½ cup currants, plumped in
hot water
¼ cup sunflower seeds, preferably
toasted
¼ cup butter
¼ cup vegetable oil
2 tablespoons honey
½ teaspoon baking soda
1 tablespoon hot water
1 egg, beaten
few drops vanilla extract

Mix oats, flour, sugar, coconut, drained currants and sunflower seeds. Heat butter, oil and honey in a small heavy-bottomed saucepan until just melted. Dissolve baking soda in hot water and add to melted mixture. Stir remaining mixture into dry ingredients. Mix well to a crumbly dough – using an electric mixer – then add egg and vanilla and continue beating until mixture forms a soft ball. Push teaspoonfuls of dough off onto lightly greased baking sheets, leaving room to spread. Bake on middle shelf of oven at 350°F for 15 minutes or until browned and firm. Cool on wire racks.
Makes about 28

ORANGE AND OATMEAL MACAROONS

1 cup soft light brown sugar
1 cup sugar
1 cup vegetable oil
2 eggs, beaten
1 cup shredded coconut
few drops vanilla extract
¼ teaspoon salt
1 teaspoon baking soda
2 teaspoons finely grated orange peel
⅓ cup chopped mixed peel
1 cup white bread flour
3½ cups oatmeal

Place ingredients in a large bowl in the order given. Mix well, then shape into a soft ball. The dough will be loose and slippery. Place teaspoonfuls on greased baking sheets, pinching gently to shape and leaving plenty of room for spreading. Bake at 350°F for 15 minutes. Stand for 1 minute to crisp. Use a spatula to transfer to wire racks to cool. Store in airtight container, with sugar sprinkled between each layer.
Makes about 80

SPICED MINCEMEAT BARS

BASE
4 cups all-purpose flour
1 tablespoon baking powder
¼ teaspoon salt
2 teaspoons ground cinnamon
1 teaspoon apple pie spice
2 cups confectioners' sugar
1 cup plus 2 tablespoons butter,
softened
2 eggs, beaten

FILLING
1 pound store-bought mincemeat
1 large Granny Smith apple, peeled
and coarsely grated
5 teaspoons brandy
extra confectioners' sugar

Sift dry ingredients. Cut in the butter, and then add eggs. (An electric mixer may be used.) Knead to a ball, wrap and freeze until firm, about 45 minutes. Remove three-quarters of the dough from the freezer and coarsely grate into a large, lightly greased square or rectangular baking pan. Pat down with your hands to form a smooth, ¼-inch thick base.
For the filling, mix mincemeat, apple and brandy, then spread evenly over dough. Remove remaining dough from freezer and grate coarsely over the top, spreading evenly with a fork. Bake at 325°F for 50 minutes or until crisp. Cut into bars and cool in pan. Dust with confectioners' sugar, remove and place on wire racks until completely cool.
Makes about 40

HONEYED SEED COOKIES

Intriguing, caramel-colored cookies, containing sunflower seeds and whole-wheat flour. The crisp sesame topping makes these singularly attractive cookies.

½ cup butter, softened
few drops vanilla extract
½ cup soft light brown sugar
5 teaspoons honey
½ cup all-purpose flour
pinch of salt
½ teaspoon baking soda
½ cup whole-wheat flour
¼ cup sunflower seeds, preferably
lightly toasted
about 3 tablespoons sesame seeds

Cream butter, vanilla, sugar and honey. Sift all-purpose flour with salt and baking soda, and mix in. Add whole-wheat flour and sunflower seeds. Beat well to make a soft dough, then shape into a ball. Pinch off small pieces and flatten between your palms. Dip tops in sesame seeds, coating thoroughly. Place on greased baking sheets, allowing room for spreading. Bake at 350°F for about 12 minutes, until browned. Allow to crisp on sheets for 1 minute before removing to a wire rack to cool.
Makes about 26

ORANGE, HONEY AND RAISIN CRISPS

Nutritious brown cookies, made with oil, honey and whole-wheat flour.

½ cup vegetable oil
5 teaspoons honey
½ cup sugar
1 teaspoon finely grated orange peel
¾ cup whole-wheat flour
⅓ cup self-rising flour
pinch of salt
½ cup shredded coconut
⅓ cup seedless raisins
1 egg, lightly beaten

Beat together the oil, honey, sugar and peel. Add flours, salt, coconut and raisins. Mix well, add egg and mix to a soft, rather oily dough. Roll into balls and place on lightly greased baking sheets. Flatten with bottom of a glass. Bake at 350°F for 15 minutes or until firm and richly browned. Cool on a wire rack. *Makes about 28*

CHOCOLATE DIGESTIVES

Serve these wholesome cookies plain or topped with chocolate.

3½ cups oatmeal
1 cup whole-wheat flour
½ cup self-rising flour
pinch of salt
4 tablespoons sugar
½ cup butter
3 tablespoons honey
about 3 tablespoons milk

TOPPING
3½ ounces semisweet chocolate
2 teaspoons water
2 teaspoons butter

Process oatmeal in a food processor fitted with grinding blade, until fairly fine, but do not grind to a flour. Mix with both flours and salt. Add sugar. Melt butter with honey over low heat – the mixture should just melt without bubbling. Slowly beat into flour mixture. Mix well, then add just enough milk to make a soft dough. Pat out onto a lightly floured board, and roll flat, about ⅛ inch thick, with a rolling pin. Using a 2½-inch cookie cutter, cut into circles. Place on greased baking sheets and prick each cookie well with a fork. Bake at 350°F for 12 minutes – watch carefully, as they brown quickly around the edges. Cool on a wire rack.

To make the topping, break up the chocolate. Add the water and butter and melt over low heat. Remove, stir until smooth, then spread the chocolate thinly over the top of each cooled cookie. Place on wire racks to set before storing. *Makes about 50*

FROM THE TOP: *Chocolate Digestives; Spiced Mincemeat Bars; Orange and Oatmeal Macaroons; Honeyed Seed Cookies.*

Caramel Squares; Featherlight Chocolate Swirls; Frosted Chocolate Squares; Clove-studded Spicy Brown Cookies.

CARAMEL SQUARES

The richest, sweetest cookies.

1 cup plus 2 tablespoons butter
¾ cup sugar
2 cups all-purpose flour
1 teaspoon baking powder
1 teaspoon ground cinnamon
3–5 tablespoons finely chopped
pecans

FILLING
1 cup canned condensed milk
5 teaspoons light corn syrup
5 teaspoons sugar
5 teaspoons water
2 tablespoons butter
few drops vanilla extract

Cream butter and sugar. Sift flour with baking powder and cinnamon and add to creamed mixture. Mix well – the dough will be very soft. Press two-thirds of the mixture evenly into a lightly greased, 13- × 8-inch jelly-roll pan. Add the nuts to the remaining third, wrap in waxed paper and place in freezer. Bake the base at 325°F for 15 minutes.

Meanwhile, make filling by placing condensed milk, syrup, sugar, water and butter in small, heavy-bottomed saucepan. Bring to a boil over low heat, stirring all the time to dissolve the sugar, and then boil gently until thick and a light caramel in color. Stir continually and take care that it doesn't scorch on the bottom as it burns very easily. Remove from heat and add vanilla, then pour over half-baked base, spreading evenly. Grate chilled dough coarsely over the top.

Bake on middle shelf of oven at 325°F for 25 minutes or until the filling is the color of fudge. Cut into squares and cool in pan before removing.
Makes about 24

> HINT
> ◉ *When measuring honey or syrup, use a measuring spoon or cup which has been greased or used to measure oil – the honey or syrup will slide out easily.*

FEATHERLIGHT CHOCOLATE SWIRLS

A light and fluffy mixture, resulting in pale, melt-in-the-mouth cookies.

½ cup butter, softened
½ cup sugar
1 egg, lightly beaten
few drops vanilla extract
1¾ cups self-rising flour
5½ tablespoons cornstarch
1½ ounces semisweet chocolate
3 tablespoons water
candied cherries

Cream butter and sugar until light. Beat in egg and vanilla. Sift flour with cornstarch and mix in. Place broken up chocolate in small container, add water, and melt over simmering water. Add to the creamed mixture and beat until thoroughly combined. Use an electric beater, and the mixture will soon become the correct consistency for piping. Fill pastry bag fitted with a star nozzle and pipe in small whirls onto baking sheets lined with waxed paper, leaving room for spreading. Press a quartered cherry into the top of each. Bake at 325°F for 20 minutes. Using a spatula, transfer to a wire rack to cool.
Makes 24–30

CLOVE-STUDDED SPICY BROWN COOKIES

These easy-to-make, economical cookies should be kept for a few days to allow the flavor to develop.

½ cup butter, softened
¾ cup sugar
1 egg, beaten
3 tablespoons light corn syrup
3 cups white bread flour
1 teaspoon baking soda
¼ teaspoon salt
1 teaspoon ground cinnamon
2 teaspoons apple pie spice
whole cloves

Cream the butter, sugar, egg and syrup together. Sift the flour, baking soda, salt and ground spices together and add. Mix into a ball, pinch off pieces, roll into small balls and place on greased baking sheets. Press a clove into the center of each. Bake on middle shelf of oven at 350°F for 12 minutes, or until lightly browned. Using a spatula, transfer to a wire rack to cool.
Makes about 40

FROSTED CHOCOLATE SQUARES

A crunchy base spread with a dark, sweet topping.

BASE
½ cup sugar
1 cup whole-wheat bread flour
1 cup shredded coconut
5 teaspoons cocoa powder
½ teaspoon baking soda
1 cup oatmeal
½ cup butter, softened
few drops vanilla extract

TOPPING
1½ cups confectioners' sugar,
sifted
2 teaspoons cocoa powder
small nut-sized piece of butter
few drops vanilla extract
hot water

In a large bowl, mix together the sugar, flour, coconut, cocoa, baking soda and oatmeal. Beat in the butter and vanilla until thoroughly combined. Press the mixture firmly into a greased 13- × 8-inch jelly-roll pan. Bake at 350°F for 20 minutes. Cut into squares and leave in pan to cool slightly before spreading with topping.

For the topping, beat confectioners' sugar, cocoa, butter and vanilla together, adding just enough hot water to make a spreading consistency – do not use too much or the frosting will not set. Spread over base and re-cut squares when set. Remove when cold.
Makes about 30 large squares

FRUIT DROPS

These are economical, spicy and wholesome chews, using oil, dried fruit and whole-wheat flour.

1 cup all-purpose flour
½ teaspoon baking powder
1 teaspoon baking soda
pinch of salt
1 teaspoon ground cinnamon
½ teaspoon grated nutmeg
pinch of ground cloves
2 eggs
⅔ cup vegetable oil
½ cup sugar
½ cup soft light brown sugar
1 cup whole-wheat flour
1 cup oatmeal
½ cup shredded coconut
1½ cups mixed dried fruit

Sift all-purpose flour, baking powder, baking soda, salt and spices. Beat eggs well with oil and both sugars. Mix into sifted mixture, then add whole-wheat flour, oatmeal, coconut and fruit. Mix well. Place teaspoonfuls on well-greased baking sheets, leaving room for spreading. Bake in the center of the oven at 350°F for 12 to 15 minutes until browned. Cool on wire racks.
Makes about 48

FIVE-STAR FRUIT SQUARES

Richly browned, sweet, cakelike bars.

2 cups self-rising flour
1 teaspoon ground cinnamon
½ teaspoon grated nutmeg
pinch of ground cloves
1 cup sugar
½ cup shredded coconut
1½ cups mixed dried fruit
¼ cup sunflower seeds, toasted
¾ cup plus 2 tablespoons vegetable oil
7 tablespoons butter, melted
2 eggs, beaten
1⅓ cups bran flakes, coarsely crushed
few drops vanilla extract

Into a large mixing bowl, sift flour with spices. Using a wooden spoon, mix in remaining ingredients, stirring well to combine.

Press mixture very firmly and evenly into a greased 10- × 8- × 2½-inch baking or small roasting pan. Bake on middle shelf of oven at 350°F for 35 minutes until risen, browned and firm – do not overbake. Cut into squares or bars and leave in pan until cool.
Makes 24 to 30

NOTE
● *If preferred, 1 cup vegetable oil may be used and the butter omitted – the texture will be less moist, rather like a cookie.*

DATE, NUT AND OATMEAL COOKIES

½ cup butter
½ cup sugar
1 egg, beaten
¾ cup pitted chopped dates
½ cup chopped walnuts or pecans
1 cup all-purpose flour or whole-wheat bread flour
½ teaspoon baking powder
½ teaspoon baking soda
pinch of salt
1 cup oatmeal
½ cup shredded coconut
few drops vanilla extract

Melt butter, add sugar and mix well. Pour into mixing bowl and add egg. Stir in dates together with walnuts or pecans. Sift flour, baking powder, baking soda and salt and add to butter mixture, returning any bran left in sifter. Add oatmeal, coconut and vanilla. Mix well – the mixture will be soft, but it firms up on cooling. Shape into small balls and place on lightly greased baking sheets, leaving room for spreading. Flatten lightly with a fork. Bake at 350°F for 12 minutes or until golden brown. Cool on wire racks.
Makes about 30

ALMOND MERINGUE FINGERS

2 egg whites
1 cup sugar
½ cup finely chopped almonds
semisweet chocolate (optional)

Beat egg whites until fairly stiff. Beat in sugar, a little at a time, and beat until mixture is stiff and glossy. Fold in almonds. Fill a pastry bag with mixture and, using a plain nozzle, pipe 3-inch long fingers onto baking sheets which have been greased and dusted with cornstarch. Bake at 275°F for 1½ hours, until pale beige in color, then turn off oven and leave until cool before opening the door. If using the chocolate finish, melt chocolate with 1 to 2 teaspoons water and dip in the end of each meringue finger, turning to coat. Place on a wire rack to set.
Makes about 20

OATMEAL AND COCONUT COOKIES

Large, crunchy cookies.

1 cup plus 2 tablespoons butter, softened
1 cup soft light brown sugar
1 cup whole-wheat bread flour
3 cups oatmeal
1 cup shredded coconut
¼ teaspoon salt
few drops vanilla extract
½ teaspoon baking soda
3 tablespoons hot water

Cream butter and sugar very well. Add flour, oatmeal, coconut, salt and vanilla. Dissolve baking soda in the hot water and add. Mix well. Roll into small balls, or push from a teaspoon into rough heaps on greased baking sheets, leaving plenty of room for spreading. Flatten lightly with a fork. Bake at 350°F for 15 minutes or until pale brown. Remove carefully, using a spatula, and leave on wire racks to crisp.
Makes about 36

Quick Fruit Bars

Dark and fruity, nutty and chewy, this recipe makes a big batch.

2 cups self-rising flour
3 cups soft light brown sugar
1½ cups shredded coconut
1½ cups mixed dried fruit
½ cup chopped pecans or toasted almonds
2 eggs
few drops vanilla extract
½ cup butter
7 tablespoons vegetable oil
1 tablespoon cocoa powder
2 teaspoons apple pie spice

In a large bowl, mix flour, sugar, coconut, fruit and nuts. Stir in eggs beaten with vanilla. Melt together the butter, oil, cocoa and apple pie spice over low heat. Add to flour and fruit mixture and mix well. Press firmly into a greased 10- × 8-inch baking pan (the batter will be rather moist and slippery, but this is correct).

Bake at 350°F for 40 minutes until firm. Cut into 24 jumbo bars or into 36 medium squares and cool in pan.
Makes 24 to 36

Chocolate-Oatmeal Refrigerator Squares

1 cup sugar
5 tablespoons cocoa powder
½ cup milk
½ cup butter
¾ cup seedless raisins
pinch of salt
3½ cups oatmeal
1 cup shredded coconut
few drops vanilla extract

Put sugar, cocoa, milk, butter, raisins and salt into heavy-bottomed saucepan. Bring to a boil over low heat, stirring constantly. Simmer for about 5 minutes, then remove from the stovetop and stir in the coconut and vanilla. Mix very well. Spoon into a shallow, buttered dish, patting mixture in to a thickness of

Lemon Sesame Snaps (page 9); Almond Meringue Fingers; Fruit Drops.

about 1 inch. Cool, then cut into 28 squares, using a knife dipped into water. Store in the refrigerator.
Makes 28

NOTE
● *When melting chocolate, be careful not to overheat it, and do not stir. If too thick for easy dipping, it may be thinned down with just a dash of boiling water and then stirred until smooth.*

GINGERBREAD MEN

Gingerbread "people" are traditional party fare and may be simply decorated with currants for eyes and buttons down the middle of the body, or more elaborately frosted after baking, using a very thin nozzle to pipe on hair, mouths, bow ties, collars, even shoes and aprons. If decorating before baking, it is important to brush the cookie with unbeaten egg white, not only to secure the currants, but to provide a shiny finish. If you do not have a gingerbread cutter, use animal shapes or any other cutters.

½ cup butter, softened
½ cup soft light brown sugar
2 tablespoons light corn syrup
1 egg, lightly beaten
2½ cups all-purpose flour
1 teaspoon baking soda
1 tablespoon ground ginger

SPECIAL DECORATIVE FROSTING
1½–2¼ cups confectioners' sugar
3 tablespoons egg white (about 1 large egg)
6 drops lemon juice

Cream butter, sugar and syrup until light and fluffy. Beat in egg. Sift flour, baking soda and ginger. Beat into creamed mixture, and when well mixed, knead lightly. Using a floured rolling pin, roll out on a lightly floured board, then cut into shapes. Arrange on greased baking sheets and apply egg white and currants. Bake on middle shelf of oven at 350°F for about 10 minutes. Leave to cool on baking sheets before transferring to wire racks.

For the frosting, sift confectioners' sugar. Using a fork, beat egg white until foamy. Slowly beat in confectioners' sugar, using a wooden spoon and beating well between additions. When a thick, piping consistency has been reached, beat in lemon juice. Pipe onto cooled gingerbread shapes as suggested, and leave on a wire rack to cool and set.

Gingerbread Men, Party Faces, gingerbread teddy bears and colorful meringue nests.

MERINGUES

Perfect meringues, pale and crisp, are not difficult to make and the following foolproof recipe may be used in a variety of different ways. With imaginative shapes and decorations, these are ideal for children's parties. To ensure success, follow the directions carefully.

4 egg whites at room temperature
12 drops lemon juice
1 cup superfine sugar
2 teaspoons cornstarch

The mixing bowl (preferably not plastic) and beaters must be spotlessly clean and free from grease. Beat egg whites with lemon juice to soft peak stage. While beating, add ¾ cup of the sugar, a little at a time, and beat until very stiff. Using a metal spoon, fold in remaining sugar and the cornstarch. (The addition of cornstarch helps to prevent "weeping.") The mixture may now be spooned into a pastry bag, or simply dropped in mounds, with a little peak to the tops, onto *ungreased* baking sheets. (Simply line with waxed paper or baking parchment – the cooked meringues will peel off very easily.) Bake meringues on the middle shelf of the oven at 250°F for 1 hour – do not open the door at all. Turn off oven and leave meringues inside until absolutely cool before removing and storing in an airtight container.
Makes about 24 small shapes

VARIATIONS
Party Meringues
If using a pastry bag, try one or more of the following ideas (none of which requires artificial food coloring) for children's parties:

● Using a plain nozzle, pipe out the letters of the alphabet.
● Pipe meringue into circles and top with chocolate sprinkles before baking. Or pipe into logs and dip one end of each baked log into melted chocolate when cool.
● Pipe into nests, and use as containers for small candies.
● Using a fluted nozzle, pipe into "caterpillars" with peaked tails. For the feelers, insert two small pieces of spaghetti and dust the body lightly with a little cocoa powder.
● For meringue mice, use a plain nozzle and pipe mixture into mounds, tapering front and back. Push two tiny segments of candied cherry into the front, for the eyes, and two short pieces of spaghetti on each side for the whiskers. Use flaked almonds for the ears, and either spaghetti or a short strip of licorice for the tail. (Some children are allergic to licorice, so spaghetti may be a better choice.)

Chocolate Meringues
Use 1 teaspoon cocoa powder for each egg white used, adding it to the sugar.

PARTY FACES

Cheerful cookies to brighten a birthday party. Made from a basic dough and cut out with a large round cutter, these may be decorated before baking, or left plain, and then frosted and decorated when cool. Use the suggestions below, or have fun fashioning your own funny faces. Artificially colored frosting is not necessary – the candies and cherries are colorful enough and look best on plain white frosting.

4 cups all-purpose flour
1 teaspoon baking powder
¼ teaspoon salt
1 cup sugar
1 cup plus 2 tablespoons butter
2 eggs
few drops vanilla extract

FROSTING
1¾ cups confectioners' sugar, sifted
1 tablespoon butter, softened
4 teaspoons boiling water

Sift flour, baking powder, salt and sugar. Cut in butter until finely crumbled. Beat eggs with vanilla and add. Mix well, then knead to a dough. Pat out on a lightly floured board and then roll out fairly thinly, using a floured rolling pin. Cut into circles with a 3-inch cookie cutter, then place on greased baking sheets, leaving room for spreading. Re-roll and cut the trimmings. If desired, decorate cookies before baking by brushing with unbeaten egg white and lightly pressing in segments of candied cherries for the eyes, a currant or chocolate morsel for the nose, and an almond sliver for the mouth. Bake on middle shelf of oven at 350°F for 12 minutes, until pale gold and just beginning to color around the edges. Transfer to a wire rack to cool.

For the frosting, combine all ingredients until smooth. Coat top of each baked cookie smoothly, using a knife dipped into boiling water. Use candies or chocolate morsels for eyes or noses, currants for eyes, licorice or almond slivers for eyebrows and mouths, and chocolate sprinkles for hair.
Makes about 40

GINGER-GLAZED SHORTBREAD

Delicious, gingery wedges, thinly covered with a fudgy glaze.

BASE
½ cup butter, softened
4 tablespoons sugar
1½ cups all-purpose flour
1 teaspoon baking powder
2 teaspoons ground ginger

GLAZE
4 tablespoons confectioners' sugar, sifted
2 tablespoons butter
½ teaspoon ground ginger
1 tablespoon preserved ginger syrup

Cream butter and sugar until light. Sift dry ingredients and add. Mix well and then knead until dough forms a ball. Pat out and press evenly into an ungreased 9-inch loose-bottomed cake pan. Prick well, press around the edge with the tines of a fork and mark into 12 wedges. Bake on middle shelf of the oven at 325°F for 40 minutes.

Just before end of baking time, prepare glaze. Combine ingredients in small saucepan. Heat very gently until just melted – on no account let mixture boil. Using the back of a spoon, spread hot mixture over hot, cooked base to within 1 inch of the edge so the crimping remains visible. Cut through wedges and leave until cool. Cut again, push up base and remove. Decorate with slivers of preserved ginger if desired.
Makes 12 wedges

COCONUT SHORTBREAD FINGERS

An unusual shortbread with a slight twist to the flavor.

1¼ cups all-purpose flour
4 tablespoons sugar
¾ cup shredded coconut
½ cup butter, softened and diced
extra sugar

Mix dry ingredients. Cut in butter thoroughly, using an electric mixer, until mixture has a fine, crumbly consistency, then knead very well until dough clings together and forms a smooth ball. Press evenly into an ungreased 9-inch square baking pan, mark into 21 fingers and prick well. Bake on middle shelf of oven at 300°F for 50 to 60 minutes. Cut through fingers, sprinkle with extra sugar and leave in pan until cool before removing. Store in an airtight container.
Makes 21

RICH SCOTS SHORTBREAD

Traditional ingredients, and the traditional method, result in this picturebook, perfect shortbread, suitable for a special occasion. To shape, use decorative shortbread molds if you have them. Dust the molds with cornstarch before pressing in the dough each time, and it will unmold easily. Alternatively, use layer cake pan, as follows.

½ cup butter, softened
3 tablespoons sugar
1 cup plus 2 tablespoons all-purpose flour
5 teaspoons rice flour

Cream the butter, then slowly beat in the sugar. When well mixed, gradually add the flour sifted with rice flour. When thoroughly combined, knead gently until mixture holds together and forms a ball. Lightly dust a 7-inch cake

pan with cornstarch. Shake out the excess, then pat the shortbread dough in firmly and evenly. Turn out onto an ungreased baking sheet by running a knife around the edges, turning the pan upside down, and giving it a hard shake. The shortbread "cake" should drop out easily. If there is any cornstarch on the top, use a pastry brush to remove. Crimp edges with forefinger and thumb, prick well and score lightly into eight wedges. Bake on middle shelf of oven at 300°F for 45 minutes until palest beige in color. Dust with a little extra sugar, cut through the wedges and leave until cool before removing.
Makes 8 wedges

SHORTBREAD PENNIES

If you don't have a wooden stamp, preferably with a thistle design, or a shortbread mold, simply prick each circle twice with the tines of a fork to resemble buttons, in which case these are called Shortbread Buttons.

1¼ cups all-purpose flour
5 teaspoons cornstarch
5½ tablespoons confectioners' sugar
½ cup butter, softened
few drops vanilla extract
sugar

Sift flour, cornstarch and confectioners' sugar. Cut in butter until mixture is very finely crumbled. Add vanilla and knead well to make a smooth dough. This takes several minutes. Pat out on an unfloured board, then roll lightly with a rolling pin to flatten evenly, ¼ inch thick. Cut into circles, using a 1½- or 2-inch cookie cutter. It is important that the circles are of uniform thickness. Gather up trimmings, knead, pat out and cut until all the dough has been used. Place circles on ungreased baking sheet and either stamp or prick as suggested. Bake at 300°F for about 30 minutes until deep gold in color. Do not allow to brown. Transfer to a wire rack and sift sugar over the shortbread while warm.
Makes 22 to 24

Ginger-glazed Shortbread; Shortbread Pennies; Melt-away Shortbread.

SPICY SHORTBREAD

This shortbread is made with oil.

1¾ cups all-purpose flour
5½ tablespoons cornstarch
pinch of salt
1 teaspoon grated nutmeg (scant)
½ cup sugar
⅔ cup vegetable oil
TOPPING
1 teaspoon sugar mixed with pinch of
ground cinnamon

Sift dry ingredients. Add oil and knead until smooth. Press dough onto the ungreased base of a 9-inch loose-bottomed cake pan. Use a rolling pin to flatten evenly. Mark into 12 wedges, prick well, crimp edges and sprinkle with topping. Leave to stand for about 30 minutes.

Bake at 300°F for 45 minutes. Cut right through wedges, but leave on base of pan until gold and crisp.
Makes 12 wedges

MOCHA-PECAN SHORTBREAD

½ cup butter, softened
4 tablespoons sugar
2 teaspoons instant coffee granules
2 teaspoons water
1¼ cups all-purpose flour
3 tablespoons cornstarch
3-5 tablespoons chopped pecans

Using an electric mixer, cream butter. Slowly add sugar, beating until light and fluffy. Beat in coffee dissolved in water. Sift flour with cornstarch and add slowly, beating all the time.

When the mixture becomes moist and forms a ball, add nuts and knead well. Press into an ungreased 7-inch square baking pan, prick well and mark into 18 fingers.

Bake on middle shelf of oven at 300°F for 45 minutes. Cut through and leave in pan until cool.
Makes 18

MELT-AWAY SHORTBREAD

A basic, failproof recipe.

1 cup plus 2 tablespoons butter,
softened
½ cup sugar
2½ cups all-purpose flour
8½ tablespoons cornstarch
extra sugar

Cream butter. Slowly add sugar, beating well until pale and fluffy. Sift flour with cornstarch and slowly beat into butter mixture to make a soft and creamy dough. Press evenly into an ungreased 13- × 8-inch jelly-roll pan.

Bake at 300°F for 45 minutes until a pale biscuit color.

Remove from oven and cut through fingers. Sprinkle lightly with sugar and leave in pan until cool. Transfer and store in airtight container.
Makes about 30

WHITE FARMHOUSE BREAD

Quick-rise yeast reduces the rising time of bread, and I have used it here to make a high, attractive flour-topped loaf. The "farmhouse" effect comes from slashing the unbaked loaf lengthwise – as it rises in the oven the slashes open out. Baked in a small bread pan, the result is a loaf with a high, humped fanlike top. However, the dough may be used in more conventional ways, if preferred.

2 teaspoons quick-rise dry yeast
4 cups white bread flour
1 teaspoon salt
1½ teaspoons sugar
2 tablespoons butter
1½ cups plus 2 tablespoons warm water

In a large bowl, mix yeast, flour sifted with salt, and sugar. Cut in butter. Add water. Mix, first with a wooden spoon and then with the hands, to make a kneadable dough, adding about 4 teaspoons extra warm water if necessary. Knead in the bowl for about 5 minutes, until soft and pliable, then cover bowl with a damp towel and leave to rest for 30 minutes in a warm place. Meanwhile, grease an 8- × 4- × 2½-inch bread pan.

Punch dough down, then form into a loaf by pressing dough out to the length of the pan, and three times the width. Fold over, sides to middle, and drop into pan, seam side down. Press dough evenly into the corners. Cover loosely with greased plastic wrap and leave to rise for 30 minutes until dough reaches just over the top of the pan. Using a sharp knife, make several deep slits lengthwise along the top of the loaf, then sift over a little flour.

Bake on middle shelf of oven at 400°F for 30 minutes until well risen and the slashes have burst open. Turn out onto a wire rack to cool.
Makes 1 loaf

Italian Herb Bread (page 39); Cheese-topped Onion Crown Loaf (page 40); White Farmhouse Bread; Baker's Pride Bread (page 39).

BASIC WHITE BREAD

Baking one's own bread is one of the ultimate culinary pleasures – from the fermenting of the yeast and the rising of the dough, to the final, aromatic waft of a crusty loaf. However, yeast breads cannot be hurried. A good rising, especially the second one, is vital.

7 cups white bread flour
2 teaspoons salt
2 tablespoons butter
2 teaspoons sugar
2½ cups warm water
1 tablespoon active dry yeast

GLAZE
1 egg white lightly mixed with 1 teaspoon water

Sift flour and salt into a large bowl. Cut in butter. Dissolve the sugar in 1 cup of the water. Sprinkle the yeast on the top, cover and leave for about 10 minutes until frothy. Make a well in center of flour mixture, pour in yeast mixture and mix, then add remaining water. Mix to a dough – you may need just a little extra water. Turn out onto a lightly floured board and knead very well, for about 10 minutes, until smooth and elastic. Brush a large bowl with oil, turn the ball of dough in it to coat, then cover and leave to rise in a warm place for about 1½ hours until doubled. (To test, press deeply with a finger – the indentation should remain.)

Punch down and knead briefly, then break off two-thirds of the dough. Knead into a loaf and place in a greased 8- × 5- × 3-inch bread pan. Brush top with glaze, cover lightly and leave for about 1½ hours or until dough reaches to ¾ inch above top of pan. Brush again with glaze. Bake at 425°F for 15 minutes. Reduce heat to 400°F and bake another 35 minutes. Turn out onto a wire rack – if you tap the bottom of the loaf, it should sound hollow. Leave on a wire rack to cool.

To make a Vienna Double Braid, roll remaining dough into six long sausage shapes of equal length. Make two braids, place one on top of the other, dampen ends and pinch to seal. Cover lightly and leave to rise for about 1½ hours until doubled. Place on a greased baking sheet, brush with milk and sprinkle with poppy seeds. Bake at 425°F for 10 minutes, then at 400°F for 20 minutes or until the bottom sounds hollow if tapped. Cool on a wire rack. Break into chunks to serve. *Makes 2 loaves*

WHITE HERB BREAD BRAIDS

For extra lightness, use half white bread flour and half all-purpose flour.

7 cups white bread flour, sifted
2 teaspoons salt
2 tablespoons butter, melted
1 small onion, finely chopped
2 cloves garlic, crushed
1 teaspoon dried thyme
2 teaspoons sugar
7 tablespoons chopped fresh parsley
about 2½ cups warm water
1 tablespoon active dry yeast
grated Parmesan cheese and poppy seeds

Sift flour with salt. Add butter, onion, garlic and herbs. Stir sugar into 1 cup of the water, sprinkle in the yeast, cover and leave to froth. Pour the yeast mixture into a well in the flour, mix and add the remaining water or enough to make a workable dough. Knead until smooth and elastic. Shape into a ball and return to bowl. Brush top with oil, cover and leave to rise in a warm place until doubled, about 45 minutes.

Punch down, knead well and then divide into two portions. Divide each half into three pieces, roll into long sausage shapes and then braid, pinching to close at both ends. Place loaves on greased baking sheets, cover lightly with damp towels and leave to rise until doubled – 30 to 60 minutes. Brush with milk and sprinkle with Parmesan cheese and poppy seeds. Bake at 425°F for 10 minutes, then reduce heat to 350°F and bake for 20 minutes longer. Cool on a wire rack.
Makes 2 large braids

POPPY SEED BRAID

This recipe makes a beautifully big, rich white braid, but it requires three risings, so allow plenty of time.

1 cup warm water
2 tablespoons sugar
2 teaspoons active dry yeast
4 cups white bread flour
1 teaspoon salt
2½ tablespoons vegetable oil
2 eggs, beaten
poppy seeds

Pour ¼ cup of the water into a small bowl. Stir in 1 teaspoon of the sugar and then sprinkle in the yeast. Cover and leave to froth. Sift flour and salt. Add remaining sugar. Quickly stir yeast mixture and pour into a well in center of flour mixture. Stir to mix, then add oil, eggs and remaining water. Mix to a workable dough – you may need a dash more water. Turn out onto a floured board and knead for 10 minutes until very smooth and pale khaki colored. Shape into a ball, brush a bowl with oil and turn dough in it until coated. Cover and leave to rise until doubled, about 1¼ hours.

Punch down, cover and leave to rise again until doubled. Divide dough into three pieces, then roll each into 16-inch long sausages, and braid. Pinch ends firmly together and place on a greased baking sheet. Cover loosely with greased plastic wrap and leave to rise until doubled, about 45 minutes. Brush top with milk and sprinkle with poppy seeds. Bake just above center of oven at 400°F for 10 minutes, then at 350°F for 20 minutes. Carefully transfer to a wire rack to cool.
Makes 1 loaf

FRENCH BREAD

Home-bakers cannot produce typical French baguettes. The technique differs from that of ordinary bread and the equipment can be quite daunting. This fairly quick-and-easy recipe, however, will produce two fine loaves, or bâtards. French bread contains no sugar, butter or oil, so eat it on the day of baking.

1 tablespoon active dry yeast
1¾ cups warm water
2¾ cups all-purpose flour
2¾ cups white bread flour
1 teaspoon salt
sesame seeds

Sprinkle yeast into ½ cup of the water, cover and leave to stand for about 15 minutes until frothy. Sift flours and salt into a large bowl. Stir the bubbly yeast and pour into a well in the center of sifted mixture. Mix and then slowly add the remaining water, making a fairly soft dough. Another 1 to 2 teaspoons water may be necessary. Knead vigorously for 10 minutes on lightly floured board. Return to bowl, cover loosely with a damp towel and leave to rise in a warm place for about 2 hours or until just more than doubled. Prod with two fingers – the indentations should remain. Punch down and knead hard for a few minutes.

Divide dough into two balls, cover and stand for 10 minutes. Roll balls into two 15-inch long sausage shapes and place on floured linen dish towel (not terry-cloth). Tuck cloth tightly up against sides to prevent loaves from spreading sideways. Cover loosely with another towel and leave to rise for 1 to 1½ hours until nearly doubled in height.

Without touching the loaves, roll them very gently onto a nonstick baking sheet so that they lie upside down. Remove any traces of flour with a pastry brush. Slash tops three times diagonally, brush with water and sprinkle with sesame seeds. For a shiny, crisp crust, place a pan of boiling water at bottom of a 425°F oven for 15 minutes. Reduce heat to 350°F and bake for 20 minutes.

Cool on a wire rack.
Makes 2 loaves

WHITE RING BREAD

Similar to the Greek kouloura ring, this is a plain but attractive loaf, baked in a ring pan. It rises into a high ring with a nice brown crust, strewn with poppy seeds.

4 teaspoons sugar
4 tablespoons warm water
2 teaspoons active dry yeast
1 cup milk
1 tablespoon butter
1 egg, beaten
3 cups white bread flour
1 teaspoon salt
poppy seeds

Dissolve 1 teaspoon of the sugar in the water, sprinkle in the yeast, cover and leave to froth. Meanwhile scald the milk, add butter and remaining sugar and cool to lukewarm. Stir in egg, reserving 1 teaspoon. Sift flour with salt into mixing bowl. Stir frothy yeast and pour into a well in the center of flour. Mix, then add milk mixture and combine well to make a very soft dough. Turn out onto well-floured board and knead for 10 minutes, adding about 4 tablespoons extra flour in stages, as it becomes necessary. When dough is smooth and pliable and no longer sticky, shape into a ball and place in a greased bowl, turning to coat. Cover and leave to rise until doubled, about 1¼ hours.

Punch down and knead for 1 minute, then roll into a long, smooth sausage shape. Coil the sausage in a greased 8-inch springform ring pan that is 3 inches deep, joining ends firmly by first brushing with a little of the reserved beaten egg. Press dough down evenly – the pan should be half full. Cover and leave until dough has risen to just over the top – about 1¼ hours. Brush top with the remaining egg and sprinkle liberally with poppy seeds. Place a pan of hot water on bottom shelf of oven, and bake bread in center of oven at 400°F for 10 minutes. Cover loosely with a sheet of aluminum foil and bake for 30 minutes longer at 350°F. Release spring of pan and turn out to cool on a wire rack.
Makes 1 loaf

ITALIAN HERB BREAD

A fragrant round loaf, baked in a cake pan. This is not a standard bread dough, and it takes longer to rise than usual, but the reward is in the eating. Break into crusty chunks, and serve warm with butter and a bowl of hot soup.

1 teaspoon sugar
4 tablespoons warm water
2 teaspoons active dry yeast
½ cup milk
2 tablespoons butter
1 egg, beaten
3 cups white bread flour
1 teaspoon salt
5 tablespoons finely chopped parsley
2–3 large cloves garlic, crushed
4 scallions, plus some of the tops, chopped
1 teaspoon dried oregano
5 teaspoons grated Parmesan cheese

Stir sugar into water, sprinkle in yeast, cover and leave to froth. Scald milk, remove from stovetop, add butter and when melted, stir in egg. Cool to luke-warm. Sift 1 heaped cup of the flour with the salt into a bowl. Stir the bubbly yeast and pour into a well in center of flour mixture. Mix and add the milk mixture. Stir in parsley, garlic, scallions and oregano. When well combined, sift in remaining flour. Mix with hands until dough holds together and then turn out onto a floured board and knead for 5 to 10 minutes until dough forms a pliable ball. Brush the bowl with oil and turn the dough in it to coat, then cover and leave until well risen, about 2 hours.

Punch down and knead lightly. Place in a greased 8-inch cake pan that is 2½ inches deep, pressing in vigorously with fingers to spread out to sides in a flat, level cake. Cover with a towel and leave to rise for 1½ hours or until dough fills two-thirds of pan. Brush with milk and sprinkle with Parmesan cheese, then bake on middle shelf at 400°F for 10 minutes, then at 350°F for 25 minutes. The loaf will sound hollow when tapped underneath. Turn out onto a wire rack to cool.
Makes 1 loaf

Italian Herb Bread and Baker's Pride Bread are both delicious with soup.

BAKER'S PRIDE BREAD

A big, savory loaf that is so easy to make, but really impressive.

4 cups white bread flour
2 teaspoons quick-rise dry yeast
1 teaspoon salt
1½ teaspoons Italian seasoning
1 small onion, finely chopped
7 tablespoons chopped parsley
2 teaspoons sugar
1 tablespoon vegetable oil
2 cups warm water
caraway seeds

Mix the flour, yeast, salt, herbs, onion, parsley and sugar in large bowl. Stir oil into water and add to flour mixture. Mix to a tacky batter, then turn into a greased 8- × 5- × 3-inch bread pan. The batter will be quite headstrong and elastic – use a damp rubber spatula to press it in evenly. Sprinkle top with caraway seeds. Leave to rise, uncovered, until dough rises to just above the top of pan – 35 to 45 minutes.

Bake at 400°F for 30 minutes, then at 350° for 30 minutes. Turn out and leave to cool on a wire rack.
Makes 1 large loaf

CHEESE-TOPPED ONION CROWN LOAF

The risen dough is shaped into balls and arranged in a cake pan for proving, where they join into a circle of rolls with humped tops.

1 teaspoon sugar
¾–1 cup warm water
1½ teaspoons active dry yeast
2 cups white bread flour
1 teaspoon salt
1 cup whole-wheat flour
1 large onion, finely chopped and sautéed in a little oil
7 tablespoons finely chopped fresh parsley
2 tablespoons butter

TOPPING
5 tablespoons finely grated Cheddar cheese
plenty of freshly ground black pepper

Stir sugar into water, sprinkle in yeast, cover and leave to froth. Sift white flour with salt. Add whole-wheat flour, onion and parsley. Cut in butter. Stir frothy yeast and pour into a well in center of dry ingredients. Mix to a dough, first with a wooden spoon and then with your hands. Turn out onto a floured board and knead for 5 minutes to a soft and elastic ball. Place in a greased bowl, turn to coat, then cover and leave to rise until doubled, about 1 hour.

Punch down, cover and rest for 10 minutes. Divide into six pieces and roll each into a smooth ball. Place five of the balls in a ring around the sides of a greased 8-inch cake pan that is 2½ inches deep, spacing them equally. Place the sixth ball in the center. Cover with greased plastic wrap and leave to rise for about 45 minutes, until rolls reach top of pan and join together.

Brush with milk, sprinkle with cheese and grind the pepper over. Bake just above center of oven at 400°F for 10 minutes, then at 350°F for 35 minutes longer. Run a knife around the circumference and turn out onto a wire rack to cool. Serve by breaking rolls apart.
Makes 1 loaf

CHEESE-AND-CARAWAY COTTAGE LOAF

This quaintly shaped loaf is lightly flavored with caraway and enriched with cheese and skim-milk powder. These two ingredients may be omitted for a lighter-textured loaf.

2 teaspoons sugar
1½ cups warm water
2 teaspoons active dry yeast
4 cups white bread flour
2 teaspoons salt
2 teaspoons dry mustard
3 tablespoons skim-milk powder
1 teaspoon caraway seeds
2½ cups finely grated Cheddar cheese

Mix sugar into water, sprinkle in yeast, cover and leave to froth. Sift flour, salt, mustard and milk powder. Add caraway seeds and 2 cups of the cheese. Stir yeast and pour into a well in center of dry ingredients. Mix well, adding about 2 teaspoons warm water to make a kneadable dough. Turn out onto lightly floured board and knead 5 to 8 minutes until smooth and elastic. Place in bowl brushed with oil, turn to coat, cover and leave to rise for 1¼ to 1½ hours until doubled. (Due to the extra ingredients this dough has a slow rising period.)

Punch down, cover and rest for 10 minutes. Pinch off three-quarters of the dough and shape it into a flat 7-inch circle, using a rolling pin to get it really level. Brush with milk. Form the remaining piece of dough into a ball and place on top of the base. Push the handle of a floured wooden spoon right through the center, from the top to the bottom, to keep top ball in place. Remove spoon and place the loaf in a greased 9-inch square pan – this prevents the base from spreading too much – then cover loosely with greased plastic wrap and leave to rise for about 45 minutes until doubled.

Brush with milk, sprinkle with remaining cheese, and bake on middle shelf of oven at 400°F for 30 minutes. Cover loosely with aluminum foil if over-browning. Cool on a wire rack.
Makes 1 loaf

SPICED FRUIT BRAID

½ cup seedless raisins
⅓ cup currants
3 tablespoons chopped mixed peel
5 teaspoons dark rum
5 teaspoons sugar
½ cup warm water
2 teaspoons active dry yeast
2¾ cups white bread flour
½ teaspoon salt
½ teaspoon apple pie spice
1 teaspoon ground cinnamon
2 tablespoons butter
1 egg, beaten

GLAZE
1 teaspoon sugar
2 teaspoons boiling water

Place fruit and rum in a bowl, stir, cover and stand for 1 hour. In another bowl, stir sugar into water, sprinkle in the yeast, cover and leave to froth.

Sift flour, salt and spices together. Cut in butter. Add egg to frothy yeast, mix well, then pour into a well in center of dry ingredients. Stir until flour is thoroughly moistened, then knead hard for 5 to 10 minutes. Cover and rest dough for 10 minutes, then add soaked fruit. At first this seems like too much fruit, but keep kneading and eventually it will all be taken up by the dough, leaving the sides of the bowl quite clean. Cover and leave to rise in a warm place until doubled, about 1½ hours.

Punch down and divide into three pieces. Roll out each portion into a 16-inch long sausage shape. Make a braid, tucking the ends under, and place on a greased baking tray. Cover lightly and leave to rise in a warm place for about 1 hour or until doubled (test by prodding with one finger – the indentation should remain).

Bake at 425°F for 10 minutes, then reduce heat to 350°F and bake for 20 minutes longer, covering the top loosely with a sheet of foil, shiny side out, when sufficiently browned. Cool braid on a wire rack and glaze while warm, not hot. To make the glaze, dissolve sugar in the water. Brush over the top of the loaf.
Makes 1 loaf

SWEDISH TEA RING

½ cup milk
3 tablespoons butter
1½ teaspoons active dry yeast
3 tablespoons warm water
3 tablespoons sugar
1 egg, beaten
1¾ cups all-purpose flour
½ teaspoon salt
FILLING
4 teaspoons butter, melted
2 tablespoons sugar
½ cup mixed dried fruit
6 candied cherries, chopped
½ teaspoon ground cinnamon
½ teaspoon apple pie spice

Scald milk, add butter and cool to lukewarm. Sprinkle yeast into warm water, cover and leave to froth. Stir sugar and egg into milk mixture. Sift flour and salt, stir frothy yeast and pour into a well in center of flour. Add milk mixture and mix to a soft dough. Knead on a floured board for 5 to 8 minutes, slowly adding extra flour as necessary until dough becomes smooth and pliable. Return to bowl, brush top with oil, cover with a damp towel and leave to rise in a warm place for about 1½ hours or until doubled.

Punch down, knead for 1 minute, then cover and leave again for 30 minutes. Roll out on a floured board to a large rectangle, about ¼ inch thick. Brush entire surface with melted butter. Sprinkle with sugar, fruit and spices, then roll up tightly, like a jelly roll. Curve into a ring, about 9 inches in diameter, joining ends firmly with dampened fingers. Lift carefully onto a greased baking sheet. Using kitchen scissors, snip top at 1¼-inch intervals, cutting half way through dough. Cover loosely with greased plastic wrap and leave until well risen, about 45 minutes.

Bake on middle shelf of oven at 400°F for 10 minutes, then at 350°F for 15 minutes. Place aluminum foil over the top when lightly browned. Leave to cool for a few minutes on the baking sheet, then transfer to a wire rack to cool completely. Frost and decorate when cool.

Makes 1 ring loaf

The colorful Swedish Tea Ring and Spiced Fruit Braid will draw many compliments.

HEALTH BREADS

Nutty Brown Bloomer Loaf

A beautiful bread, incorporating two flours, wheat germ and sunflower seeds. This requires only one rising, which is quite lengthy due to the unrefined ingredients, but it is nevertheless easy to make and is tops on the taste test.

3 cups whole-wheat flour
2 teaspoons salt
1 tablespoon quick-rise dry yeast
1½ cups warm water
5 teaspoons honey
5 teaspoons vegetable oil
2 cups white bread flour
3 tablespoons wheat germ
2½ cups sunflower seeds

In a large bowl, combine 1½ cups of the whole-wheat flour, salt and rapid-rise yeast. Mix water, honey and oil. Stir into flour mixture and mix to a sloppy dough. Cover and rest for 10 minutes. Add remaining whole-wheat flour, the white flour, wheat germ and sunflower seeds. Mix with a wooden spoon and then with your hands to form a dough, adding up to 5 tablespoons extra warm water as necessary. Knead in the bowl for 8 to 10 minutes – this is a firm dough which requires some hard kneading. When mixture forms a smooth ball and leaves the sides of the bowl clean, shape into a 10- × 5-inch thick roll with blunt ends.

Place on a greased baking sheet, and tuck two cloths tightly on each side so that the dough rises upward, rather than sideways. Make six deep diagonal slashes across the top, cover loosely with greased plastic wrap and leave to rise for 1 hour or until doubled. Brush with milk and bake on middle shelf of oven at 400°F for 30 minutes until loaf sounds hollow when tapped. Cool on a wire rack, and brush top with melted butter for a shiny finish.
Makes 1 loaf

FROM THE BACK: *Nutty Brown Bloomer Loaf; Caraway Rye Loaf; Brown Herb Bread Braid; Buttermilk Whole-wheat Soda Bread with Rosemary.*

Brown Herb Bread Braid

This is a rewarding bread to bake, rising beautifully to a fat and chunky braid, topped with cracked wheat and lightly flavored with herbs. The addition of a little soybean flour is optional, but it adds nutrition and helps to keep the loaf fresh. Break into chunks to serve.

1¼ cups warm water
2 teaspoons active dry yeast
2 cups white bread flour
2 cups whole-wheat flour
3 tablespoons soybean flour (optional)
2 teaspoons Italian seasoning
1 teaspoon salt
5 teaspoons vegetable oil
5 teaspoons honey

TOPPING
2 tablespoons cracked wheat
¼ teaspoon Italian seasoning

Pour ½ cup of the water into a small bowl. Sprinkle in yeast, cover and leave to froth. Mix white bread, whole-wheat and soybean flours in large bowl. Add herbs, salt, oil and honey. Stir the risen yeast and pour into a well in center of dry ingredients. Add remaining water, or just enough to make a workable dough. Turn out onto floured board and knead well for 10 minutes, reflouring the board when necessary – the dough is inclined to be sticky. When the dough forms a smooth ball, place it in a bowl brushed with oil, turn to coat, cover and leave in a warm place to rise until doubled, about 1 to 1½ hours.

Punch down, cover and rest for about 10 minutes. Divide into three pieces and roll into 14-inch long sausage shapes. Make a braid, pinching ends to seal firmly. Cover loosely with greased plastic wrap and leave to prove until doubled, about 45 minutes.

Brush top with milk and sprinkle with wheat and herbs. Bake just above center of oven at 400°F for 10 minutes, then at 350°F for 20 minutes longer. Cool on a wire rack.
Makes 1 loaf

Whole-wheat Batons with Garlic and Fresh Herbs

These French-style batons are excellent with soups, cheese or pâté.

2 teaspoons honey
1¼ cups warm water
2 teaspoons active dry yeast
2 cups white bread flour
1 teaspoon salt
2 cups whole-wheat flour
4 cloves garlic, crushed
3 tablespoons finely chopped fresh parsley
1 teaspoon chopped fresh rosemary leaves
10 fresh sage leaves, chopped
1 teaspoon finely chopped fresh oregano leaves, or ½ teaspoon dried
beaten egg, sesame and poppy seeds

Dissolve honey in water. Sprinkle in yeast, cover and leave to froth. Sift white flour with salt into a large bowl. Add whole-wheat flour, garlic and all the herbs and mix well. Pour frothy yeast into a well in center and work in the flour until incorporated. Turn out onto a lightly floured board and knead hard for 10 minutes. Shape into a ball, return to bowl, brush top with oil, cover and leave to rise in a warm place for about 1½ hours or until doubled.

Punch down and divide into two pieces. Shape each piece into an 11-inch long roll and place on a greased baking sheet. With a sharp knife, slash the tops three times, diagonally. Leave to rise until nearly doubled, about 1¼ hours. Brush with beaten egg and sprinkle with sesame and poppy seeds in alternate, diagonal stripes. Bake just above center of oven at 425°F for 10 minutes, then at 350°F for 15 minutes longer. Cool on a wire rack.
Makes 2 loaves

> HINT
> • *Remember to remove the greased plastic wrap on top of a risen loaf before baking.*

WHOLE-WHEAT NUT, RAISIN AND YOGURT BREAD

A superb, nutritious snacktime loaf.

1 cup white bread flour
1 teaspoon salt
1½ teaspoons baking soda
1 teaspoon ground cinnamon
½ teaspoon grated nutmeg
¼ teaspoon ground cloves
3 cups whole-wheat flour
1½ tablespoons vegetable oil
1½ tablespoons honey
3 tablespoons soft light brown sugar
½ cup seedless raisins
about ½ cup finely chopped walnuts,
pecans or Brazil nuts
2¼ cups plain yogurt

TOPPING
½ teaspoon ground cinnamon
1½ tablespoons soft light brown sugar

Sift white flour with salt, baking soda and spices. Mix in whole-wheat flour, oil, honey, sugar, raisins and nuts. Stir in yogurt, using a wooden spoon. Rinse the carton with 5 teaspoons water and add. Mix all the ingredients very well, then turn the batter into a greased 9- × 5-× 3-inch bread pan, spreading evenly.

Sprinkle cinnamon and sugar over the top. Bake on middle shelf of oven at 350°F for 1 hour. Let stand for 5 minutes before turning out onto a wire rack to cool.
Makes 1 loaf

HINT
◉ *Baking bread with a pan of water placed low down in the oven will produce a crisp crust.*
◉ *Be wary of adding too much water to a batter bread. If you make it too wet, the loaf will deflate in the oven. The consistency should be fairly thick and moist, almost like a fruit cake batter.*

WHOLE-WHEAT HONEY BREAD

1 tablespoon rapid-rise dry yeast
2 tablespoons wheat germ
4 cups whole-wheat flour
½ cup seedless raisins
1 teaspoon salt
¼ cup sunflower seeds
about 2¼ cups warm water
2 tablespoons honey
1 tablespoon vegetable oil

Mix yeast, wheat germ, flour, raisins, salt and sunflower seeds in a large mixing bowl. Beat 1 cup of the water with honey and oil. Pour into the dry ingredients and mix, then add remaining water, or enough to make a batter with the consistency of a fruit cake. Turn the batter into a greased 8- × 5- × 3-inch bread pan, and cover loosely with greased plastic wrap. Leave in a warm place until batter rises to just over the top of the pan – about 30 minutes.

Bake at 400°F for 30 minutes, then reduce heat to 350°F and bake for 20 minutes longer. Turn out onto a wire rack to cool.
Makes 1 large loaf

BUTTERMILK WHOLE-WHEAT SODA BREAD WITH ROSEMARY

Soda bread is a traditional Scottish bread, served on Burns Night with Finnan Haddie Soup and haggis. I have flavored this with fresh rosemary. Serve freshly baked, broken into quarters, with butter.

2 cups all-purpose flour
1 teaspoon salt
1 teaspoon baking soda
1 teaspoon sugar
2 cups whole-wheat flour
1 tablespoon finely chopped fresh
rosemary leaves
2 tablespoons butter
about 1¾ cups buttermilk

Sift all-purpose flour with salt and baking soda. Add sugar, whole-wheat flour and rosemary. Cut in butter. Add buttermilk and mix to a soft dough. Shape into two 6-inch rounds, and place on a floured baking sheet. Using the back of a knife, score deeply into quarters. Brush tops with beaten egg (milk may be used, but egg gives a better color).

Bake at 400°F for 30 minutes.
Makes 2 loaves

ENRICHED BATTER BREAD

A delicious, healthy loaf.

1½ tablespoons honey
2 cups warm water
2 teaspoons active dry yeast
3 cups whole-wheat flour
5 tablespoons cracked wheat
5 tablespoons soybean flour
5 tablespoons nonfat milk powder
2 tablespoons wheat germ
1 cup whole-wheat bread flour
1½ teaspoons salt
1½ tablespoons vegetable oil
sunflower seeds

Dissolve honey in ½ cup of the water. Sprinkle in the yeast, cover and leave to froth. Mix the remaining ingredients, except sunflower seeds. Give the yeast a quick stir and pour into a well in center of the dry ingredients. Mix, using a wooden spoon, and gradually add the remaining water, or just enough to give you a thick, sticky batter. Turn batter into a greased 9-× 5-× 3-inch bread pan, making it nearly two-thirds full. Sprinkle the top thickly with sunflower seeds, pressing them in lightly. Cover loosely with greased plastic wrap and leave to rise in a warm place for 45 to 60 minutes.

Bake on middle shelf of oven at 400°F for 15 minutes, then at 350°F for 45 to 60 minutes. Stand for a few minutes before running a knife around edges. Leave to cool on a wire rack.
Makes 1 loaf

PUMPERNICKEL BREAD

This is an unusual dark bread made with a variety of flours and interesting ingredients which can include mashed potato, caraway seeds, chocolate and coffee powder. The following is a delectable, fairly sweet version, containing a sprinkling of fruit, honey and molasses, with the cocoa and coffee providing color rather than flavor.

1¼ cups warm water
1½ tablespoons molasses
3 tablespoons honey
2 teaspoons active dry yeast
2 teaspoons instant coffee granules
2 teaspoons salt
1 tablespoon cocoa powder

1½ tablespoons butter, melted
2 cups rye flour
1½ cups white bread flour
1 cup whole-wheat flour
3 tablespoons seedless raisins
3 tablespoons currants

GLAZE
1 egg white mixed with 2 teaspoons water

In a large bowl, mix water, molasses and honey. When dissolved, sprinkle in yeast, cover and stand until batter begins to bubble, about 15 minutes. Stir in coffee, salt, cocoa and butter and when smoothly mixed, add the flours, one by one. Mix to a dough, turn out onto a lightly floured board and knead vigorously for 10 minutes until smooth and pliable. Place in a bowl brushed with oil, turn to coat on all sides, then cover bowl with plastic wrap, leaving plenty of room for air and rising. Leave the dough in a warm place until nearly tripled in bulk, 2 to 2½ hours. To test, prod with one finger and if the indentation remains, it is ready.

Punch down, add raisins and currants and knead hard for 5 minutes. Shape into a large round, place on a greased baking sheet which has been dusted with cornstarch. Cover lightly and leave to rise for 1½ to 2 hours, until doubled. Brush with glaze. Bake at 400°F for 50 to 60 minutes. The bread will be dark and shiny, and should sound hollow when tapped on the bottom. Cool on a wire rack and serve cut into thin slices. *Makes 1 large loaf*

Whole-wheat Nut, Raisin and Yogurt Bread, a superb, nutritious snacktime loaf to serve with cheese, cold meats or pâté.

CARAWAY RYE LOAF

*Good with cheese, cold meats,
mustard and pickles.*

1½ tablespoons molasses
¾ cup warm water
2 teaspoons active dry yeast
1 cup white bread flour
1 cup whole-wheat flour
1¼ cups rye flour
1 teaspoon salt
1½ tablespoons vegetable oil
1 teaspoon caraway seeds

Dissolve molasses in water. Sprinkle in yeast, cover and leave to froth. Meanwhile, mix remaining ingredients, except caraway seeds. Stir bubbly yeast and pour into a well in center of dry ingredients. Mix to a dough. You might have to add 1–2 tablespoons extra warm water. Turn out onto a lightly floured board and knead for 10 minutes until smooth. The dough will be firm, rather than spongy. Brush a bowl with oil and turn the ball of dough around in it until coated, then cover and leave to rise for about 1½ hours until doubled.

Punch down and knead in caraway seeds until well distributed. Shape into 9-inch long loaf, and place on a greased baking sheet. Make three deep diagonal slashes on the top, then cover loosely with greased plastic wrap and leave to rise for about 45 minutes or until doubled – the dough will "fatten" up by rising both upward and sideways. Either brush top with milk and sprinkle with extra caraway seeds, or sift over a little rye flour.

Bake on middle shelf of oven at 400°F for 10 minutes and then at 350°F for 25 to 30 minutes longer. Turn out onto a wire rack to cool.
Makes 1 loaf

NOTE
● *Doughs containing rye flour are always a little sticky.*
● *If bread dough has risen before the oven is ready, immediately place in a cool place and uncover.*

CHEESE, ONION AND GARLIC BATTER BREAD

2 teaspoons rapid-rise dry yeast
1½ cups white bread flour
1½ cups whole-wheat flour
1 teaspoon salt
2 teaspoons sugar
2 cloves garlic, crushed
3 tablespoons finely grated Cheddar cheese
1 small onion, finely chopped
3 tablespoons chopped fresh parsley
2 tablespoons butter
about 1½ cups warm water
sesame seeds

Mix yeast, both flours, salt, sugar, garlic, cheese, onion and parsley. Cut in butter. Stir in water, using just enough to make a thick, oatmeal-like batter. Turn the batter into a greased 8- × 4- × 2½-inch bread pan, sprinkle with sesame seeds, and drape a piece of greased plastic wrap very lightly over the top. Leave in a warm place for about 30 minutes or until doubled.

Bake at 400°F for 30 minutes, then again at 350°F for 30 minutes. When the loaf is sufficiently browned, cover lightly with a sheet of aluminum foil. Let stand for a few minutes, then turn out and then return to oven, upside down, for 5 minutes to crisp the sides. Cool on a wire rack.
Makes 1 loaf

INSTANT WHOLE-WHEAT BATTER BREAD

The perfect bread for reluctant bakers.

3 cups whole-wheat flour
1 cup white bread flour
4 tablespoons cracked wheat
2 teaspoons rapid-rise dry yeast
1 teaspoon salt
¼ cup sunflower seeds
1½ tablespoons vegetable oil
1½ tablespoons honey
about 2 cups warm water
extra sunflower seeds

Mix dry ingredients. Mix in oil and honey. Add 1¼ cups of the water, then stir in just enough of remaining water to make a soft, sticky dough. Mix well, then turn into a greased 9- × 5- × 3-inch bread pan, sprinkle with sunflower seeds, pressing in lightly. Leave to rise in a warm place until ½ to ¾ inch over top of pan. Cover, if you like, with a large plastic bag, allowing it to balloon over the top so it does not stick to the rising dough.

Bake on middle shelf of oven at 400°F for 30 minutes and then at 350°F for 20 minutes longer. Turn out and leave to cool on a wire rack.
Makes 1 medium loaf

FOUR SEED BATTER BREAD

This loaf slices well.

1½ tablespoons honey
2¼ cups warm water
1 tablespoon active dry yeast
4 cups whole-wheat flour
1 cup white bread flour
3 tablespoons sesame seeds
¼ cup sunflower seeds
4 tablespoons poppy seeds
1 teaspoon salt

Mix honey into 1 cup of the warm water and stir to dissolve. Sprinkle in the yeast, cover and leave to froth. Mix flours, sesame seeds, sunflower seeds, 3 tablespoons poppy seeds and salt. Stir risen yeast, pour into a well in center of flour mixture and stir, then slowly add remaining water, or just enough to make a sticky, quite stiff dough. Pat firmly into a greased 9- × 5- × 3-inch bread pan, sprinkle with remaining poppy seeds. Leave to rise in a warm place for 1 hour, or until just over the top of the pan. Bake at 400°F for 30 minutes, and then at 350°F for 30 minutes longer. Run a knife around the sides and leave in pan for 1 minute before turning out onto a wire rack to cool.
Makes 1 loaf

Oatmeal Batter Bread With Herbs

1 teaspoon sugar
about 1½ cups warm water
2 teaspoons active dry yeast
1¾ cups whole-wheat flour
¾ cup white bread flour
1 cup cracked wheat
1 cup oatmeal
1 teaspoon salt
3–4 cloves garlic, crushed
1½ tablespoons finely chopped fresh
rosemary leaves
1½ tablespoons vegetable oil
1½ tablespoons honey

Stir sugar into 1 cup of the water, sprinkle in the yeast, cover and leave to froth, about 15 minutes. Mix flours, cracked wheat, oatmeal, salt, garlic and rosemary. Stir oil and honey into yeast mixture, then add to flour mixture. Mix, then slowly stir in remaining water, or enough to make a sloppy batter. When well combined, turn into a greased, 8- × 4- × 2½-inch bread pan. Smooth the top, then leave in a warm place until dough rises ½ inch over the top of the pan — about 45 minutes. Bake at 400°F for 30 minutes, then at 350°F for 20 to 25 minutes longer. Stand bread in pan for 1 minute, then run a knife around the edges and turn out onto a wire rack to cool. Brush top with melted butter.
Makes 1 loaf

Nutty Whole-wheat Batter Bread

Excellent with pâtés or cheese.

2¼–2½ cups warm water
1 tablespoon honey
2 teaspoons active dry yeast
4 cups whole-wheat flour
1 cup white bread flour
1½ teaspoons salt
1 tablespoon vegetable oil
¼ cup sunflower seeds
4 tablespoons poppy seeds
extra sunflower seeds

A crunchy slice of Instant Whole-wheat Batter Bread or Nutty Whole-wheat Batter Bread goes well with a crisp salad.

Mix 1 cup of the water with the honey and stir until dissolved. Sprinkle yeast on top, cover and leave until frothy, about 10 minutes. Mix whole-wheat and white flours, salt and oil. Stir in yeast mixture, sunflower and poppy seeds. Add rest of water, or just enough to make a soft dough. Spoon into a greased and floured 8- × 5- × 3-inch bread pan, patting in firmly. Sprinkle the top with extra sunflower seeds and leave to rise in a warm place for about 1 hour, or until dough rises to ¾ inch above the top of the pan. Bake at 400°F for 45 minutes. Run a knife around the edges, then turn out and leave to cool on a wire rack.
Makes 1 fairly large loaf

ROLLS

White Rolls

2 teaspoons sugar
½ cup warm water
2 teaspoons active dry yeast
½ cup milk
1 tablespoon milk
1 tablespoon butter
4 cups all-purpose flour
1 teaspoon salt
1 egg, beaten

Stir sugar into water, sprinkle in yeast, cover and leave to froth. Scald milk, add butter and leave until lukewarm. Sift flour and salt together. Stir yeast, pour into a well in center of flour, and mix. Beat egg into cooled milk mixture and add all at once to flour mixture. Mix to a kneadable dough, adding about 1½ tablespoons extra warm water if necessary. Turn out onto a lightly floured board and knead for 10 minutes until pliable and smooth. Shape into a ball, put back in greased bowl, turn to coat, cover and leave to rise for 1 to 1½ hours until doubled.

Punch down, cover and leave to rest for 5 to 10 minutes. Shape as required. Place on a greased baking sheet and leave to prove for 30 to 40 minutes until virtually doubled. Brush with milk, and sprinkle with suggested toppings. Bake just above the center of oven at 425°F for 10 minutes, then at 350°F for 5 minutes. (Brushing with milk provides a light golden color; egg-wash may be used, but be careful of overbrowning.) *Makes 12 large rolls*

Rolls

Roll into balls. Brush with milk and sprinkle with poppy or sesame seeds before baking.

FROM THE BACK: *Baking Powder Rolls; Quick Cheese Crescents; White Rolls in three different shapes.*

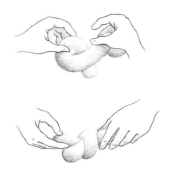

Knots

Tie 12-inch long sausage shapes of dough into loose knots.

Cloverleaf Rolls

Pinch off pieces of dough, divide into three pieces and form into small balls. Push together to join. May also be dropped into muffin pans.

Cottage Rolls

Pinch off pieces of dough and divide each piece into two-thirds and one-third. Roll the larger pieces into balls, then place on greased baking sheets and brush with milk. Roll the smaller pieces into balls and place on top. Dip your finger into flour, then push right through the two balls.

Bridge Rolls

Shape dough into small sausage shapes and place close together in a baking pan. Before baking, sift flour over the tops. Break apart once baked.

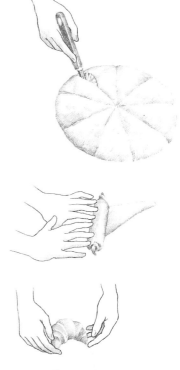

Crescents

Roll a piece of dough into a circle and cut into triangles. Roll up from long end and twist into crescent shapes.

Braids

Pinch off pieces and divide each into three pieces. Roll into 8-inch long sausage shapes. Brush with milk and sprinkle with sesame seeds before baking.

VARIATION
Rosemary Rolls

For a different flavor, add a large sprig of finely chopped rosemary leaves to the flour, and before baking brush tops of rolls with milk and sprinkle with crushed dried rosemary.

CROISSANTS

2 teaspoons sugar
3 tablespoons warm water
1 tablespoon active dry yeast
½ cup milk
½ cup water
1 egg, separated
3 cups plus 2 tablespoons all-purpose flour
1 teaspoon salt
¾ cup plus 2 tablespoons butter
egg white, or an extra yolk beaten with 1 teaspoon water

Stir sugar into 3 tablespoons water, sprinkle in yeast, cover and leave to froth. Scald milk and water, then leave until lukewarm. Beat egg yolk, then stir in cooled milk-water. Stir yeast and add. Sift ¾ cup of the flour with the salt and add. Beat to combine, using a wooden spoon, then give a quick beat with an egg mixer to smooth out lumps.

Sift remaining flour and, using two knives, or your fingertips, cut or rub in butter until particles are the size of peas. Pour liquid into a well in the center, and mix lightly with a wooden spoon until flour is thoroughly moistened and sticky. Push together with a spatula, cover with a damp towel, and leave to rise in a warm place until doubled – about 1¼ hours – then refrigerate, covered, until well chilled, 1½ to 2 hours.

Turn out onto a floured board and knead very lightly with floured fingertips for a few minutes, until smooth. Cut dough into three portions and, using a floured rolling pin, roll each into a 10- to 12-inch circle. Cut across into six or eight triangles. Starting at the wide outer edge, roll each triangle inward. Place, with points facing down, on greased baking sheets. It is important to allow plenty of room for rising and spreading. Twist slightly into crescent shapes, cover loosely with lightly greased plastic wrap and leave to rise until doubled, about 45 minutes. The tops may be brushed with reserved egg white, but egg-wash gives a better golden color. Bake just above center of oven at 425°F for 15 minutes. Serve hot, with butter or jam.
Makes 18–24

VARIATIONS
Chocolate croissants
After cutting the triangle of dough, place two squares of semisweet chocolate spaced slightly apart, along wider outer edge, then roll up as usual.
Whole-wheat croissants
Make as above, except for the following changes: use 3½ ounces warm water instead of 3 tablespoons, and 1 cup all-purpose flour and 2 cups whole-wheat flour. Sift all-purpose flour with the salt and add to the milk-water mixture. Beat as before. Place whole-wheat flour into a bowl and rub or cut in butter. Then proceed with the mixing and chilling as above. After cutting and shaping, the dough will need a slightly longer rising period until croissants have doubled. Brush with egg-wash and bake as for plain croissants.

MUFFIN PAN WHOLE-WHEAT ROLLS

A basic whole-wheat batter is used for these wholesome, quickly made muffin-shaped "rolls."

2¼ cups warm water
pinch of sugar
2 teaspoons active dry yeast
3 cups whole-wheat flour
1 cup white bread flour
½–1 cup seedless raisins (optional)
⅓ cup oatmeal
1 teaspoon salt
1½ tablespoons vegetable oil
1½ tablespoons honey or half honey, half molasses
½ cup sunflower seeds
extra sunflower or sesame seeds or cracked wheat

Mix 1 cup of the water with a pinch of sugar, sprinkle in yeast, cover and leave to froth. Mix remaining ingredients, except sunflower or sesame seeds or cracked wheat, in large bowl. Stir yeast and pour into a well in center of dry ingredients. Mix, and then slowly stir in remaining warm water, or just enough to make a thick, moist dough. Spoon into large greased muffin pans – they should be just over halfway filled with batter. Top with extra sunflower or sesame seeds, or cracked wheat, pressing in lightly. Cover pan lightly with greased plastic wrap and leave to rise in a warm place until batter rises, slightly humped, to just over the tops of the pan – about 50 to 60 minutes. Bake just above center of oven at 400°F for about 25 minutes until browned and firm. Let stand for a few minutes, then run a knife around the edges to loosen. Cool on a wire rack, and eat freshly baked.
Makes 14 to 16 large rolls

BAKING POWDER ROLLS

Although baking powder rolls are not as light as yeast rolls, they are really useful when time is short, and delicious served freshly baked. The dough may be shaped into round balls, braids, finger rolls or crescents, but this version is particularly crusty.

2 cups all-purpose flour
½ teaspoon salt
4 teaspoons baking powder
2 teaspoons sugar
¾ cup milk
1 cup water
1 tablespoon butter
extra soft butter, milk and poppy seeds

Sift the flour, salt and baking powder together. Add the sugar. Gently heat the milk, water and butter together, just until butter has melted. Add to dry ingredients. Mix quickly to a soft dough, pat out ½ inch thick on a floured board, then cut into circles, using a 3-inch cutter. Make an indentation down the center of each, using the back of a knife. Spread with a little soft butter, and then fold one half over the other. Brush with milk and sprinkle with poppy seeds. Place on a greased baking sheet, cover with a cloth and let stand for 5 minutes. Bake just above center of oven at 425°F for 15 to 20 minutes, depending on size of rolls.
Makes about 10

FETA CHEESE AND GARLIC ROLLS

Beautiful little packages, with a surprise in the middle. These may be gently reheated if made in advance.

1 teaspoon sugar
about 1½ cups warm water
2 teaspoons active dry yeast
3 cups all-purpose flour
1 teaspoon salt
4 teaspoons butter, melted
7 ounces feta cheese
2 teaspoons dried oregano
4 cloves garlic, crushed
beaten egg and ground black pepper

Stir sugar into ½ cup water, sprinkle in yeast, cover and leave to froth. Sift flour and salt. Stir yeast and pour into a well in center of flour. Mix, then add remaining water, or enough to make a workable dough. Knead for 10 minutes on a floured board until creamy and smooth. Shape into a ball, brush a bowl with oil, turn dough around in bowl to coat, then cover and leave to rise for 1¼ hours or until doubled.

Punch down, cover and leave to rest for 5 minutes. Roll out thinly on a floured surface. Spread with butter and cut into 16 squares. Cut feta into 16 cubes and toss with oregano and garlic until coated. Place one cube in center of each square of dough, then fold corners to the centre and pinch points tightly to seal. Place on greased baking sheets and cover loosely with greased plastic wrap. Leave until well risen, about 1 hour. Brush with egg, and grind black pepper over the tops. Bake just above the center of the oven at 425°F for 15 minutes. Serve hot.
Makes 16

HINT
● *If bread dough does not rise, it is usually because the liquid added was either too hot or too cold. Yeast is "tougher" than one thinks – the liquid should be warmer than lukewarm.*

Slab Rusks (page 53); Whole-wheat Rusks (page 52).

QUICK CHEESE CRESCENTS

3 cups all-purpose flour
1 tablespoon baking powder
1 teaspoon salt
1 teaspoon dry mustard
1 teaspoon sugar
2 tablespoons butter
¾ cup finely grated, sharp Cheddar cheese
⅔ cup milk
⅔ cup water

TOPPING
melted butter
3 tablespoons grated Cheddar cheese
or
1 tablespoon grated Parmesan cheese
paprika

Sift flour, baking powder, salt and mustard together. Add sugar and cut in butter. Mix in the cheese. Mix milk with water and add, mixing quickly and lightly to make a soft but rollable dough. Divide into two, and roll out thinly on a lightly floured board into two 12-inch circles.

Cut each circle across into eight triangles. Roll up each triangle from the long side toward the point. Curve the dough slightly into horseshoe shapes and arrange on floured baking sheets. Bake just above the center of the oven at 400°F for 15 minutes. Remove from the oven and brush with melted butter, then sprinkle with Cheddar or Parmesan cheese, as preferred, and lightly dust with paprika. Return to the oven and bake for 5 minutes longer.
Makes 16

PITA BREADS

Much experimenting has resulted in what are, to my mind, quite the best of homemade pitas. The shaping is quite different from that of ordinary bread rolls; they rise in the oven like fat little pillows, and form perfect pockets for stuffing. A high baking temperature is important, and to ensure the formation of pockets, the dough should not be creased when rolling, or pinched when turned over just prior to baking.

2 teaspoons sugar
1¼ cups warm water
2 teaspoons active dry yeast
4 cups all-purpose flour
1 teaspoon salt
2 tablespoons vegetable oil

Stir sugar into water. Sprinkle in yeast, cover and leave to froth. Sift flour and salt into large bowl. Add oil. Stir bubbly yeast and pour into a well in center of dry ingredients. Using a wooden spoon, combine, then mix with your hands, adding about 2 tablespoons extra water, or enough to make a kneadable dough. Turn out onto a lightly floured board and knead well for 10 minutes until it forms a pliable ball. Return to bowl, brush top with oil, cover and leave to rise for about 1 hour or until doubled.

Punch down and pinch off ten equal pieces. Roll into balls and leave to rest for 5 minutes. Using a rolling pin, roll into thin ovals. Place on ungreased baking sheets dusted with all-purpose flour. Leave to rise, uncovered, for about 30 minutes, until puffy and doubled in thickness. Turn over carefully and sift a little flour over the tops. Bake, one tray at a time, just above center of oven at 475°F for 7 minutes. Remove and wrap in a cloth to soften. Cut a small slice off the edge and press sides gently to open out the pockets.
Makes 10

VARIATION
Whole-wheat pitas
Use equal quantities of white bread flour and whole-wheat flour. Sift white flour with salt, add whole-wheat flour, then proceed as for white pitas. A little extra water may be necessary, but the times rising are about the same.

WHOLE-WHEAT RUSKS

Wholesome rusks, delicious for dunking.

9 cups whole-wheat flour
2 cups white bread flour
1 cup plus 2 tablespoons sugar
1 teaspoon salt
2 teaspoons baking powder
1 teaspoon baking soda
1 teaspoon cream of tartar
1 cup plus 2 tablespoons butter, melted
¾ cup seedless raisins
2 cups buttermilk
2 eggs
¾ cup plus 2 tablespoons vegetable oil

In a large bowl, mix flours, sugar, salt, baking powder, baking soda and cream of tartar. Stir in butter and raisins. Beat buttermilk, eggs and oil. Stir into dry mixture, and knead into a dough. Roll into balls about twice the size of a golf ball. Pack closely into two base-lined and greased 8- × 5- × 3-inch bread pans. Bake at 350°F for 1 hour. Turn out and leave until cool enough to handle, then break apart, nick in half, and then carefully break again – use a knife to help, but rusks should always be broken, never sliced. Arrange loosely on baking sheets and dry out at 250–275°F. They taste even better toasted slightly.
Makes about 72

Pita Breads form perfect pockets for stuffing with cheese, cold meats or salad.

Bran Flake-Buttermilk Rusks

4 cups self-rising flour
1 teaspoon salt
1 teaspoon baking powder
½ cup sugar
2 cups bran flakes
½ cup seedless raisins
½ cup butter, melted
1 egg
1 cup buttermilk
3 tablespoons vegetable oil

Sift flour, salt and baking powder. Add sugar, bran flakes and raisins. Mix in butter. Beat egg, buttermilk and oil together and add all at once to flour mixture. Mix to soft dough, then knead well until raisins are incorporated and dough forms a ball, leaving sides of mixing bowl clean. Pinch off pieces and roll into 16 balls. Place close together in a greased and base-lined 9- × 5- × 3-inch bread pan.

Bake at 350°F for 1 hour. When tops are browned, after about 40 minutes, cover with a sheet of waxed paper. When cooked, turn out and leave until cool before breaking apart with the help of a sharp knife. Nick the tops and bottoms with a sharp knife and carefully break into two. Place on baking sheets and dry out at 225°F until crisp.
Makes 32

Aniseed-Milk Rusks

Light, white rusks which rise like cumulus clouds.

1 cup milk
½ cup water
½ cup butter
½ cup sugar
1½ tablespoons vegetable oil
1 egg, beaten
1 teaspoon malt vinegar
9 cups self-rising flour
1 teaspoon cream of tartar
1 teaspoon salt
1 teaspoon aniseed

Put milk, water, butter and sugar into a saucepan and heat while stirring, just until sugar has dissolved and butter has melted. Do not overheat. Remove from heat and add oil, egg and vinegar. Sift flour, cream of tartar and salt. Stir in the warm milk mixture and mix to a dough, adding a dash of water if necessary. Add aniseed and knead to a smooth and pliable dough. Shape into balls, about twice the size of a golf ball, and pack closely together into one large or two small greased and base-lined bread pans.

Bake for 15 minutes at 400°F, then at 350°F for 45 to 60 minutes longer, depending on size of pan used. Place a sheet of waxed paper over the top when sufficiently browned. When baked, turn out, break apart and then nick and break each ball into three or four long rusks. Arrange on baking sheets and dry out at 225°F.
Makes about 72

Buttermilk Rusks

These can also be enjoyed as a delicious type of biscuit: turn the just-baked roll-loaf out, break apart and serve hot with butter and honey.

3¼ pounds self-rising flour
2 teaspoons salt
1 cup sugar
1⅔ cups butter
2 cups plus 2 tablespoons buttermilk
3 eggs

Mix flour, salt and sugar in a large mixing bowl. Cut in the butter (if in a hurry, this may be melted instead). Mix well. Beat buttermilk with eggs and add. Knead well – the more you knead, the higher they'll rise. If the dough seems a little dry, rinse the buttermilk carton with a little water and add to the mixture to make a medium-soft but never slippery dough. Continue kneading until the dough forms a ball and leaves the sides of the bowl clean, then roll into balls about twice the size of golf balls and pack them closely into two base-lined, greased and floured 9- × 5- × 3-inch bread pans. Bake at 400°F for 30 minutes, then reduce heat to 350°F and bake for 30 minutes longer. Turn out and break apart and then, with the help of a knife, break into rusks. Arrange the rusks in single layers on baking sheets and dry out at 250°F or in a warming drawer.
Makes 84 to 96

Slab Rusks

Definitely the easiest rusks to make – the dough is simply patted out flat into a large jelly-roll pan, cut into fingers and baked.

4 cups white bread flour
1 teaspoon salt
2 teaspoons cream of tartar
1 teaspoon baking soda
½ cup sugar
½ cup butter
1 egg
1 cup buttermilk

Sift flour, salt, cream of tartar and baking soda. Mix in sugar. Rub in butter with fingertips until finely crumbled. Beat egg with buttermilk, add to flour mixture and combine, first with a wooden spoon and then with your hands until all the flour is gathered up and mixture forms a soft ball. Pat out into a 13- × 8-inch jelly-roll pan with fairly high sides. Flour hands lightly if necessary and press out evenly, spreading right into the corners. Slice into 11 or 13 strips across and 3 strips down, making 33 or 39 fingers.

Bake just above center of oven at 400°F for 30 minutes. Cut through again, then remove and arrange on baking sheets. Dry out at 250°F.
Makes 33 or 39

VARIATION
Whole-wheat rusks
Sift 2 cups white bread flour, salt, cream of tartar and baking soda. Add 2 cups whole-wheat bread flour, then proceed as above.

QUICK
BREADS

CORN BREAD

Baked in a square pan, cut into squares and served hot, this is popular with fried chicken, or at barbecues or brunches. May also be served with jam and butter.

1½ cups all-purpose flour or white bread flour
1 teaspoon salt
4 teaspoons baking powder
2 teaspoons sugar
1½ cups fine cornmeal
1 egg
1¼ cups milk
3 tablespoons vegetable oil

Sift flour, salt, baking powder, sugar and cornmeal. Beat together egg, milk and oil. Pour into a well in center of dry ingredients and mix lightly and quickly, as for muffins. Pour into a greased 9-inch square baking pan, spreading evenly and lightly with a spatula.

Bake just above center of oven at 425°F for 20 minutes until golden brown. Cut into 16 squares and cool slightly before removing from pan.
Makes 16 squares

BUTTERMILK-HERB BREAD

A wonderfully quick loaf with a tantalizing aroma.

4 cups self-rising flour
1 teaspoon dried oregano
1 teaspoon dried thyme
1 teaspoon salt
1 teaspoon sugar
7 tablespoons finely chopped fresh parsley
2 cloves garlic, crushed
half a bunch scallions, chopped
2 cups buttermilk
3–4 tablespoons water
grated Parmesan cheese and sesame seeds

FROM THE BACK: *Beer Bread; Feta Cheese and Garlic Rolls (page 51); Corn Bread; Irish Soda Bread (page 56).*

Mix flour, dried herbs, salt, sugar, parsley, garlic and onions. Stir in the buttermilk. Rinse carton with water and add, mixing well to make a sticky dough. Spoon into a greased and floured 8- × 5- × 3-inch bread pan. Smooth top, and sprinkle with cheese and sesame seeds.

Bake at 350°F for 1 hour. Run a knife around the sides, then turn out onto a wire rack. Cool slightly. Serve freshly baked with butter.
Makes 1 loaf

SAVORY CHEESE SODA BREAD

The unusual combination of onion, carrot, herbs and cheese makes an aromatic, golden-brown loaf – a marvelous variation on the Irish soda bread theme.

1 cup white bread flour
½ teaspoon salt
½ teaspoon baking soda
½ teaspoon cream of tartar
1 cup whole-wheat bread flour
1 tablespoon butter
1 medium onion, coarsely grated
¾ cup coarsely grated carrot
½ teaspoon Italian seasoning
3 tablespoons chopped fresh parsley
⅓ cup finely grated Cheddar cheese
about ¾ cup buttermilk
milk and extra cheese or sesame seeds

Sift white bread flour, salt, baking soda and cream of tartar. Mix in whole-wheat flour and cut in butter. Mix in onion, carrot, herbs, parsley and cheese. Add just enough buttermilk to form a soft dough. Mix lightly and then pat and toss mixture together to shape into a round. Place on floured baking tray and, using the back of a knife, score deeply into eight triangles. Brush with milk and sprinkle with extra cheese or sesame seeds.

Bake on middle shelf of oven at 400°F for 30 minutes. Transfer to a wire rack, but serve very fresh, broken into triangles.
Makes 1 round loaf

BAKING POWDER BREAD

4 cups white bread flour
4 teaspoons baking powder
1 teaspoon salt
2 teaspoons sugar
3 tablespoons butter
2 cups milk
2 cups water

Sift flour, baking powder and salt. Add sugar. Cut in butter until finely crumbled. Mix milk and water and add, mixing quickly to a soft dough. You might have to add about 2 teaspoons extra water. Do not knead, but pat it about until it holds together, then pat out flat into a rectangle and roll up like a jelly roll. Place, seam side down, in a greased 8- × 4- × 2½-inch bread pan. Brush with milk.

Bake toward the top of the oven at 425°F for 45 minutes until a golden brown. Turn out onto a wire rack and leave to cool.
Makes 1 loaf

BEER BREAD

Add chopped mixed fresh herbs, crushed garlic or cheese, if you wish.

3 cups self-rising flour
1 cup whole-wheat flour
½ teaspoon salt
2 teaspoons sugar
5 tablespoons finely chopped fresh parsley
1½ cups bottled beer (unchilled)
sesame seeds

Mix dry ingredients, including parsley. Stir in beer, and mix well to a tacky, springy dough. Turn into a greased base-lined 8- × 4- × 2½-inch bread pan, level top and sprinkle with sesame seeds.

Bake at 350°F for 1 hour 10 minutes, then turn out onto wire rack, remove lining paper and cool. This loaf will not be browned when baked, but rises well and has a crisp, humped crust. Any leftovers are good toasted.
Makes 1 loaf

IRISH SODA BREAD

My favorite version of this bread, with none of that overt taste of baking soda. Quantities are easily doubled to make one large or two small loaves.

1 cup white bread flour
1 cup all-purpose flour
½ teaspoon salt
½ teaspoon baking soda
½ teaspoon cream of tartar
1 tablespoon butter
about 1 cup buttermilk
beaten egg

Sift flours with salt, baking soda and cream of tartar. Cut in butter. Add 1 scant cup buttermilk all at once and mix quickly to make a soft dough, adding the extra 1½ tablespoons only if further moistening is necessary. Turn out onto a floured board and shape into a 6-inch cake. Place on a floured baking sheet and score top deeply into quarters, using the back of a knife. Brush with beaten egg.

Bake on middle shelf of oven at 400°F for 30 minutes. Serve freshly baked.
Makes 1 loaf

CHEESE, ONION AND NUT BREAD

This is a super, fairly dense and crunchy savory loaf which takes only a few minutes to mix.

3 cups self-rising flour
2 tablespoons untoasted wheat germ
1 teaspoon salt
1 teaspoon sugar
3 cloves garlic, crushed
1 medium onion, coarsely grated
¾ cup finely grated Cheddar cheese
½ cup finely chopped toasted walnuts or pecans
1 cup buttermilk
½ cup water
paprika

Mix together flour, wheat germ, salt, sugar, garlic, onion, cheese and nuts. Stir in buttermilk and water and mix to a thick and sticky batter. Turn batter into a greased 8- × 5- × 3-inch bread pan and level top with a spatula. Sprinkle with paprika. Bake on middle shelf of oven at 350°F for 1 hour. Turn out and cool on a wire rack.
Makes 1 medium loaf

PLAIN BAKING POWDER COB

Makes one small, crusty cob – a most useful quick bread that is delicious served freshly baked.

1½ cups all-purpose flour
½ teaspoon salt
4 teaspoons baking powder
1 cup whole-wheat flour
¾ cup plus 2 tablespoons milk
1 egg
extra flour or milk and poppy seeds

Sift plain flour, salt and baking powder. Add whole-wheat flour. Beat milk and egg and add. Mix to a dough, and knead lightly until it holds together. Pat into a 6-inch cake and place on floured baking sheet. Make three diagonal slashes across the top, and sift a little flour over, or brush with milk and sprinkle with poppy seeds.

Bake just above center of oven at 425°F for 20 to 25 minutes. Transfer to a wire rack. Break into chunks to serve.
Makes 1 small loaf

BUTTERMILK SCONE BREAD

Serve this delicious, quickly made bread, broken into chunks, with butter and marmalade for a leisurely Sunday breakfast.

4 cups self-rising flour
1 teaspoon salt
1 tablespoon sugar
2 tablespoons butter
about 1¾ cups buttermilk
milk, sesame and poppy seeds

Sift flour with salt. Add sugar and cut in butter. Make a well in the center of the flour mixture and pour in enough buttermilk to make a soft dough. Turn out onto a floured board and knead very lightly while patting out to an 8-inch round, rather like a giant biscuit. Place on a greased baking sheet and cut a fairly deep cross on the top. Brush each quarter with milk and then sprinkle alternate quarters with sesame and poppy seeds.

Bake on middle shelf of oven at 425°F for 10 minutes, then reduce heat to 350°F and bake for 30 minutes longer.
Makes 1 round loaf

NOTE
● *Whole-wheat and white flours can often be interchanged; however whole-wheat flour will need more liquid.*

ZUCCHINI BREAD

A large, spicy loaf that is delicious served sliced and buttered.

3 eggs
1 cup vegetable oil
1 cup sugar
few drops vanilla extract
11 ounces zucchini
2 cups all-purpose flour
(half whole-wheat bread flour
may be used)
1 teaspoon baking soda
1 teaspoon baking powder
½ teaspoon salt
1 teaspoon ground cinnamon
1 teaspoon apple pie spice
¼–½ chopped pecans or walnuts

Beat eggs, oil, sugar and vanilla together until light. Trim, pare and coarsely grate zucchini and stir in. Sift dry ingredients together and add. Finally stir in nuts. Mix well and turn into a greased, base-lined and floured 9- × 5- × 3-inch bread pan. Bake at 350°F on middle shelf of oven for 1 hour to 1 hour 10 minutes. Cool for 5 minutes, then turn out onto a wire rack, remove lining paper and leaving to cool completely.
Makes 1 loaf

A Cheese, Onion and Nut Bread slices well. Break an Irish Soda Bread in chunks.

BROWN FRUIT LOAF

1½ cups mixed dried fruit
1 cup soft light brown sugar
1 cup water
3 tablespoons vegetable oil
¼ teaspoon grated nutmeg
1 teaspoon ground cinnamon
½ teaspoon ground ginger
¼ teaspoon salt
⅓ cup chopped walnuts, pecans or
Brazil nuts
½ cup plain yogurt
1 egg
1 teaspoon baking soda
2 cups whole-wheat bread flour
1 teaspoon baking powder
few drops vanilla extract

Put dried fruit mixture, sugar, water, oil, spices and salt into a saucepan. Bring to a boil and simmer for 5 minutes. Cool thoroughly. Add nuts. Beat yogurt, egg and baking soda together, and add to fruit mixture alternately with flour. Finally add baking powder and vanilla. Spoon into a greased and floured 8- × 4- × 2½-inch bread pan and smooth top with the back of a spoon dipped into hot water.

Bake at 325°F for about 45 minutes. Turn out and cool on a wire rack.
Makes 1 loaf

COFFEE-GLAZED NUTMEG LOAF

Topped with flavored glacé icing and attractively decorated, this enticing, spicy loaf looks just as good as it tastes.

2 cups all-purpose flour
1 teaspoon baking powder
2 teaspoons grated nutmeg
pinch of salt
1 cup soft light brown sugar
½ cup butter, softened
¾ cup plus 2 tablespoons buttermilk
1 egg
1 teaspoon baking soda
½ cup chopped Brazil nuts, lightly toasted
few drops vanilla extract

GLAZE
½ cup confectioners' sugar, sifted
1 teaspoon instant coffee granules
2–3 teaspoons water
blanched almonds and cherries to decorate

Sift flour, baking powder, nutmeg and salt. Add sugar, then cut in butter until mixture is like fine bread crumbs. (A hand-held electric mixer is ideal.) Beat buttermilk with egg and baking soda. Stir into flour mixture, then add nuts and vanilla. Mix well and turn into a greased and base-lined 8- × 4- × 2½-inch bread pan. Spread evenly, smoothing top with the back of a spoon dipped into hot water.

Bake at 350°F for 1 hour. Turn out onto a wire rack, remove lining paper and cool. Turn right side up to glaze.

For the glaze, mix confectioners' sugar, coffee and enough water to make a mixture that will just pour. Glaze top of loaf, allowing it to run down the sides. When set, decorate with almond "flowers" centered with cherries. Serve sliced, with or without butter.
Makes 1 loaf

FRUIT AND CARROT LOAF

This recipe makes two medium-sized, deliciously moist loaves.

1½ cups mixed dried fruit
2½ cups water
2 cups soft light brown sugar
1½ cups coarsely grated carrots
2 tablespoons butter
2 teaspoons apple pie spice
2 cups all-purpose flour
2 teaspoons baking soda
2 teaspoons baking powder
¼ teaspoon salt
2 cups whole-wheat flour
1 cup chopped walnuts or pecans (optional)

Place fruit, water, sugar, carrots, butter and spice in a wide-bottomed saucepan, bring to a boil. Cover and simmer for 10 minutes. Cool completely.

Sift all-purpose flour with baking soda, baking powder and salt, then stir into cooled mixture. Mix in whole-wheat flour – the batter will be soft. Add nuts, if using. Turn into two greased and base-lined, or nonstick, 8- × 4- × 2½-inch bread pans. Bake at 325°F for 1 hour. Test with a skewer, and if baked through, remove from oven and leave to stand for 5 minutes before turning out onto a wire rack and removing lining paper. Leave to cool.
Makes 2 loaves

DATE LOAF

1½ cups finely chopped pitted dates
2 tablespoons butter
1 cup soft light brown sugar
½ teaspoon baking soda
1 cup boiling water
2 cups white bread flour
(half whole-wheat bread flour may be used)
pinch of salt
1 teaspoon baking powder
few drops vanilla extract
½ cup chopped walnuts (optional)

Put dates into a bowl with butter and sugar. Sprinkle with baking soda and pour boiling water over. Leave to cool, stirring occasionally. Sift flour, salt and baking powder. Add cooled date mixture. Add vanilla and nuts and mix well. Pour into a greased and base-lined 8- × 4- × 2½-inch bread pan. Level top with the back of a spoon dipped into hot water. Bake at 325°F in the center of the oven for 1 hour. Turn out onto a wire rack, remove lining paper and cool.
Makes 1 loaf

> HINT
> ● *When measuring honey or syrup, use a measure that has been oiled, or used to measure oil.*

NUTTY DARK GINGERBREAD

Satisfying and pleasantly spicy. Serve sliced and buttered.

1 cup soft light brown sugar
½ cup butter
1½ tablespoons syrup or honey
1½ tablespoons molasses
3 tablespoons milk
3 tablespoons water
1 cup whole-wheat bread flour
1 cup white bread flour
¼ teaspoon salt
¼ teaspoon grated nutmeg
1 tablespoon ground ginger
1½ teaspoons baking powder
½ teaspoon baking soda
½ cup chopped walnuts or pecans
1 egg, beaten

Heat the sugar, butter, syrup or honey, molasses, milk and water gently. Mix remaining ingredients, except egg. Pour hot, melted mixture into dry ingredients and mix well. Stir in egg. The mixture should be soft. Pour into a greased and floured 8- × 4- × 2½-inch bread pan. Bake at 350°F for about 45 minutes. Cool on a wire rack.
Makes 1 loaf

SPICED HONEY LOAF

This honey loaf is a large, spicy loaf with coffee to provide the rich brown color, and a scattering of brandy-soaked fruit. After baking, it may be topped with glacé icing and studded with blanched almonds. Serve sliced and buttered.

¾ cup mixed dried fruit, including
some candied cherries
2 large knobs preserved ginger in
syrup, chopped
1½ tablespoons brandy
3 cups all-purpose flour
1 tablespoon baking powder
½ teaspoon baking soda
¼ teaspoon salt
1 tablespoon ground ginger
1 teaspoon ground cinnamon
large pinch ground cloves
1 cup soft light brown sugar
2 eggs
7 tablespoons golden honey
1 tablespoon instant coffee granules
1 cup water
½ cup vegetable oil

Place dried fruit and ginger in small bowl. Add brandy, cover and let stand for at least 1 hour. Sift flour, baking powder, baking soda, salt and spices. Add sugar. Beat eggs until light, then beat in honey, the coffee dissolved in the water, and the oil. Add to flour mixture and mix well until thoroughly combined. Fold in fruit and turn into base-lined and greased 9- × 5- × 3-inch bread pan.

Bake on middle shelf of oven at 350°F for 1¼ hours. Test with a skewer, then let stand in pan for a few minutes before turning out onto a wire rack and removing lining paper. Leave to cool.
Makes 1 very large loaf

> HINT
> ● *Lightly toasting nuts before use brings out the flavor. Chop nuts, then spread them out on a baking sheet and place in a medium oven until lightly browned.*

FROM LEFT TO RIGHT: Date Loaf; Bran-Fruit Loaf; Fruit and Carrot Loaf.

BRAN-FRUIT LOAF

1⅓ cups bran flakes
¾ cup soft light brown sugar
¾ cup mixed dried fruit
1 cup milk
¼ cup vegetable oil
½ cup all-purpose flour
1 tablespoon baking powder
¼ teaspoon salt
1 teaspoon apple pie spice
⅓ cup finely chopped pecans
(optional)
few drops vanilla extract

Place bran flakes, sugar, fruit, milk and oil in large bowl. Stir until combined and then let stand for 30 minutes. Sift flour, baking powder, salt and spice. Add to fruit mixture, together with nuts, if using, and vanilla. Mix well, using a wooden spoon. Turn into a greased and base-lined 8- × 4- × 2½-inch bread pan.

Bake on middle shelf of oven at 350°F for 1 hour, then test with a skewer. If baked, let stand for a few minutes before turning out onto a wire rack and removing lining paper. Leave to cool.
Makes 1 loaf

CHOCOLATE, CARROT AND GINGER LOAF

This is quite different from the ordinary carrot loaf; it is large, dark and economical, with an unusual combination of ingredients. Serve sliced and buttered, rather than iced.

1 cup all-purpose flour
3 tablespoons cocoa powder
1 teaspoon apple pie spice
1 teaspoon baking soda
1 teaspoon baking powder
pinch of salt
1 cup whole-wheat flour
¾ cup seedless raisins
3 knobs preserved ginger in syrup, chopped
½ cup shredded coconut
2 eggs*
1 cup soft light brown sugar
½ cup vegetable oil
1½ cups coarsely grated carrots
few drops vanilla extract

Sift the all-purpose flour, cocoa, spice, baking soda, baking powder and salt together. Add the whole-wheat flour, raisins, ginger and coconut. Beat eggs, sugar and oil. Add to flour mixture, and when combined, stir in carrots and vanilla. Mix to a fairly stiff, sticky batter. Turn into a greased and base-lined 8- × 5- × 3-inch bread pan, smooth top with the back of a spoon dipped into hot water.

Bake on middle shelf of oven at 350°F for about 1 hour 10 minutes – test with a skewer. Let stand for a few minutes before turning out onto a wire rack and removing lining paper. Leave to cool.
Makes 1 loaf

*It is important to use extra-large eggs.

FRUIT TEA LOAF

This is just one good version of the ever-popular fruit loaf using cold tea.

3 cups mixed dried fruit
2 tea bags
2 cups boiling water
1½ tablespoons vegetable oil
2 eggs, lightly beaten
1½ cups soft light brown sugar
3 cups self-rising flour
¼ teaspoon salt
1 teaspoon ground cinnamon
1 teaspoon apple pie spice
1 teaspoon baking powder
few drops vanilla extract

Put fruit and tea bags into bowl. Pour boiling water over, stir and leave overnight.

Next day turn mixture into large mixing bowl, remove tea bags, and add oil, eggs and sugar, mixing well. Sift flour, salt, spices and baking powder. Add to fruit mixture, mix well, then stir in vanilla. Turn mixture, which will be thick and sticky, into two greased and base-lined 8- × 4- × 2½-inch bread pans. Level tops with the back of a spoon dipped into hot water.

Bake on middle shelf of oven at 350°F for 1 to 1¼ hours – test with a skewer to make sure they are baked through. Turn out onto a wire rack, remove lining paper and leave to cool. Serve sliced and buttered.
Makes 2 loaves

COCONUT-YOGURT LOAF

All the measuring is conveniently done in the yogurt carton for this large, moist loaf.

6-ounce carton plain yogurt
1 carton sugar
1 carton vegetable oil
3 eggs
few drops vanilla extract
3 cartons self-rising flour
2 cartons shredded coconut

Beat yogurt, sugar, oil, eggs and vanilla until thick and creamy. Add flour, one carton at a time, mixing well. Add coconut and mix to a very soft batter. Pour into a greased and base-lined 9- × 5- × 3-inch bread pan.

Bake on middle shelf of oven at 325°F for 1¼ hours. Let stand for a few minutes, then turn out onto a wire rack. Remove lining paper and leave to cool.
Makes 1 loaf

GLAZED LEMON LOAF

Light, lovely and lemony.

½ cup butter, softened
¾ cup sugar
finely grated peel of 1 lemon
2 cups white bread flour plus 2 teaspoons extra
2 teaspoons baking powder
pinch of salt
½ cup finely chopped mixed peel
2 eggs
1 cup milk
few drops vanilla extract

GLAZE
3 tablespoons sugar
3 tablespoons fresh lemon juice

Cream butter, sugar and lemon peel until light. Sift flour, baking powder and salt. Add mixed peel. Add eggs to creamed mixture, one by one, adding 1 teaspoon flour with each egg. Fold in flour mixture. Add milk and vanilla. Beat to a soft batter. Pour into a greased and base-lined 8- × 5- × 3-inch bread pan and smooth top with back of a spoon dipped into hot water. Bake at 350°F for 1 hour.

Just before end of baking time, make glaze by mixing sugar and lemon juice in small saucepan. Stir over low heat to dissolve sugar and then boil over high heat for 1 minute. Remove baked loaf from oven, prick the top all over with a thin skewer, and slowly drizzle lemon syrup over. Let stand in pan until cool, then run a knife around the edges, turn out and remove lining paper.
Makes 1 loaf

FROM THE BACK: *Coconut-Yogurt Loaf; Chocolate, Carrot and Ginger Loaf; Glazed Lemon Loaf.*

ONE-BOWL ORANGE LOAF

A great standby when time is at a premium – assemble the ingredients and whip up this loaf in a matter of minutes.

2 cups all-purpose flour or white bread flour
¾ cup sugar
2 teaspoons baking powder
pinch of salt
½ cup vegetable oil
½ cup fresh orange juice
1 teaspoon finely grated orange peel
2 eggs
few drops vanilla extract

GLAZE
1½ tablespoons orange juice
1 tablespoon butter
1½ cups confectioners' sugar, sifted

Sift flour, sugar, baking powder and salt. Add oil, juice and peel. Using an electric mixer, mix for 1 minute on medium speed. Add eggs and vanilla. Beat for 45 seconds or just until mixed. Pour into a base-lined, greased and floured 8- × 5- × 3-inch bread pan.

Bake at 325°F on middle shelf of oven for 1 hour. Let stand for 5 minutes, then turn out, remove lining paper and cool on a wire rack.

To make the glaze, heat orange juice and butter in small saucepan. Add confectioners' sugar and stir over very low heat until smooth. Pour over top of cool loaf, allowing glaze to trickle down the sides. Decorate loaf with cherries and orange slices.
Makes 1 loaf

HINT
● *Be wary of adding too much water to a batter bread. If you make it too wet, the loaf will deflate in the oven. The consistency should be fairly thick and moist, like a fruit-cake mixture.*

One-bowl Orange Loaf; Banana Loaf; Zucchini Bread (page 57).

Pumpkin, Pecan and Raisin Loaf

A spicy, caramel-colored loaf.

2 cups white bread flour
1 teaspoon baking powder
½ teaspoon salt
1 teaspoon ground cinnamon
1 teaspoon ground ginger
large pinch of ground cloves
⅓ cup finely chopped pecans
⅔ cup seedless raisins
7 tablespoons butter, softened
1 cup soft light brown sugar
2 eggs
1½ cups smooth pumpkin purée
1 teaspoon baking soda
1½ tablespoons water

Sift the flour, baking powder, salt and spices together. Add nuts and raisins. Cream butter and sugar. Add eggs one at a time, beating well. Mix in pumpkin purée, and then add flour mixture. Continue beating until combined. Dissolve baking soda in the water and stir into batter. Turn into a greased and base-lined 8- × 5- × 3-inch bread pan.

Bake at 350°F for 1 hour. Let stand for 5 minutes before turning out onto a wire rack and removing lining paper. Leave to cool.
Makes 1 loaf

Banana Loaf

A reliable old favorite.

2 cups white or whole-wheat bread flour
2 teaspoons baking powder
¼ teaspoon baking soda
¼ teaspoon salt
1 teaspoon ground cinnamon
½ cup butter, softened
1 cup sugar
2 eggs
4 large, ripe bananas, mashed
½ cup chopped walnuts
few drops vanilla extract

Sift flour, baking powder, baking soda, salt and cinnamon together. Cream the butter and sugar until light. Add the eggs one at a time, beating well between additions and adding 1 teaspoon of the flour mixture with each egg. Add flour mixture to creamed mixture alternately with bananas, beating well until smooth. Stir in nuts and vanilla. Pour the batter into lightly greased and base-lined 9- × 5- × 3-inch bread pan. Smooth top with the back of a spoon dipped into hot water.

Bake at 350°F for 50 to 60 minutes. Turn out, remove paper and cool on a wire rack. Serve sliced and buttered.
Makes 1 loaf

Buttermilk-Fruit Loaf

Economical and easy-to-make, rather like a light slab fruit cake. Served sliced and buttered.

3 cups self-rising flour
1 teaspoon ground cinnamon
¼ teaspoon grated nutmeg
¼ teaspoon salt
1⅓ cups mixed dried fruit
1½ cups buttermilk
1 egg
3 tablespoons honey
5 tablespoons sugar
7 tablespoons vegetable oil
cherries and blanched almonds

Sift the flour, spices and salt together. Mix in fruit. Beat buttermilk, egg, honey, sugar and oil together. Add to flour mixture and combine lightly but thoroughly. Turn into a base-lined and greased 9- × 5- × 3-inch bread pan and level top with back of a spoon dipped into hot water. As the batter is fairly stiff, cherries and almonds may be arranged on the top.

Bake on middle shelf of oven at 350°F for 1 hour. Stand for 1 minute before turning out onto a wire rack and removing lining paper. Leave to cool.
Makes 1 loaf

Surprise Loaf

This colorful tea loaf combines two vegetables in a most unusual and delicious way. Serve sliced and buttered.

7 ounces oil
1 cup sugar
2 eggs
¼ cup sunflower seeds (preferably toasted)
¾ cup coarsely grated carrots
⅔ cup peeled and coarsely grated beet
1 cup all-purpose flour
½ teaspoon salt
1 tablespoon baking powder
1 teaspoon ground cinnamon
½ teaspoon apple pie spice
1 cup whole-wheat flour

Beat oil and sugar until creamy, then add the eggs and beat well. Mix in sunflower seeds, carrots and beet. Sift all-purpose flour, salt, baking powder and spices and add to creamed mixture. Fold in whole-wheat flour. Turn into a greased and base-lined 9- × 5- × 3-inch bread pan.

Bake at 350°F for 1 hour. Let stand for 1 minute, then turn out onto a wire rack, remove lining paper and cool.
Makes 1 loaf

BASIC MUFFINS

Plain, golden muffins, delicious with butter and cheese, honey or jam.

1½ cups all-purpose flour
1 tablespoon baking powder
¼ teaspoon salt
3 tablespoons sugar
4 tablespoons vegetable oil
1 egg, beaten
½ cup milk
½ cup water

Sift flour, baking powder and salt. Add sugar. Beat together the oil, egg, milk and water. Pour all at once into well in center of dry ingredients. Mix lightly and quickly – use a wooden spoon and do not beat. Spoon into a greased muffin pan, filling two-thirds full.

Bake at 400°F for 20 to 25 minutes. Cool slightly, loosen with a knife and remove. Serve as soon as possible.
Makes about 12

APPLE, RAISIN AND HONEY MUFFINS

1 cup white bread flour
1 teaspoon ground cinnamon
¼ teaspoon grated nutmeg
small pinch of ground cloves
¼ teaspoon salt
1 tablespoon baking powder
1 cup whole-wheat flour
1 egg
3 tablespoons vegetable oil
½ cup water
½ cup milk
3 tablespoons soft light brown sugar
3 tablespoons honey
2 medium Golden Delicious apples
⅓ cup seedless raisins

Basic Muffins; Apple, Raisin and Honey Muffins.

Sift white flour, spices, salt and baking powder. Mix in whole-wheat flour. Beat together the egg, oil, water, milk, sugar and honey. Make a well in center of dry ingredients and pour in the liquid ingredients. Add peeled and coarsely grated apples, and raisins. Stir quickly until just combined – do not beat. Spoon into a greased muffin pan, filling three-quarters full.

Bake at 400°F for 20 minutes. Run a knife around the edges to loosen, and cool on a wire rack. Serve buttered.
Makes 12 to 14

FAVORITE FRUIT MUFFINS

Flop-proof, nutritious, sweet and spicy muffins which rise perfectly. These are great for lunch boxes. Chopped nuts may be added with the sugar if desired.

1 cup boiling water
¾ cup mixed dried fruit
2 tablespoons butter
1 cup white bread flour
1 teaspoon baking powder
1 teaspoon baking soda
¼ teaspoon salt
1 teaspoon apple pie spice
½ teaspoon ground cinnamon
1 cup whole-wheat flour
⅓ cup soft light brown sugar
few drops vanilla extract

Pour water over fruit and butter in a bowl and let stand for 10 minutes, stirring once to melt butter. Sift white flour, baking powder, baking soda, salt and spices. Add whole-wheat flour and sugar. Pour fruit mixture into well in center of dry ingredients and mix together with vanilla until combined – do not overmix. Spoon into a greased muffin pan, filling three-quarters full.

Bake at 400°F for 15 to 18 minutes until richly browned and firm. Run a knife around the edges to remove, then cool on a wire rack. Serve freshly baked, with butter.
Makes 12 to 14

PROCESSOR HERB MUFFINS

Fragrant with herbs and made in a jiffy, these muffins are splendid served hot from the oven with a bowl of soup. The amount of herbs is approximate – there is no need to count little leaves and sprigs meticulously – let the given quantities merely act as a guide. The important factor is to use fresh herbs.

4 sprigs fresh marjoram
2 sprigs fresh thyme
about 24 fresh rosemary needles
8 large fresh sage leaves
few fresh sprigs parsley
2 cups all-purpose flour
1 tablespoon baking powder
¼ teaspoon salt
1 teaspoon sugar
1 large clove garlic, chopped
2 scallions, plus some tops, chopped
1 egg
¼ cup vegetable oil
¾ cup plus 2 tablespoons milk
grated Cheddar cheese

Strip leaves from marjoram and thyme and place in food processor fitted with grinding blade, together with the rosemary, sage, parsley, flour, baking powder, salt, sugar, garlic and scallions. Process until herbs are finely chopped. Place in mixing bowl. Beat egg with oil and milk. Pour into a well in center of flour mixture and mix very quickly to a soft batter. Pour into a well-greased muffin pan, making about two-thirds full. Sprinkle with the cheese.

Bake at 400°F for 20 to 25 minutes. Let stand for a few seconds and then run a knife around the edges to loosen. Serve hot, with butter.
Makes 12 muffins

SCALLIONS, CHEESE AND CELERY MUFFINS

Marvelously aromatic, golden-brown, light muffins. These are super with soup.

2 cups self-rising flour
½ teaspoon dry mustard
¼ teaspoon salt
¼ cup butter
2 large stalks celery
4 scallions, plus some of the tops, chopped
3 tablespoons grated Cheddar cheese
1 egg
1 cup buttermilk
Paprika

Sift the flour, mustard and salt together. Cut in the butter until finely crumbled. Grate the celery coarsely and squeeze dry with paper towels if necessary. Add to dry mixture together with onions and cheese. Beat egg with buttermilk and add. Mix quickly and lightly. Spoon the butter into a greased muffin pan, filling two-thirds full. Lightly dust tops with paprika.

Bake at 400°F for 20 to 25 minutes. Leave to stand for about 1 minute before removing. Serve warm with butter.
Makes 12

GREEN PEPPER AND ONION MUFFINS

Aromatic, savory muffins.

1 egg
3 tablespoons vegetable oil
½ cup low-fat cream cheese
7 tablespoons milk
7 tablespoons water
2 cups all-purpose flour
1 tablespoon baking powder
½ teaspoon salt
4 tablespoons finely chopped green pepper (discard all seeds and core)
6 scallions, chopped
½ teaspoon Italian seasoning
12-16 small cubes of Gouda cheese

Beat the egg, oil, cream cheese, milk and water together. Sift flour, baking powder and salt together. Add to liquid mixture, stir until just combined, then add green pepper, onions and herbs. Mix quickly and lightly. Spoon into greased muffin pans, filling two-thirds full. Top each with a cube of Gouda.

Bake on middle shelf of oven at 400°F for 25 minutes. Run a knife around the edges to loosen, and remove.
Makes 12–16

HINT
● *If your bread loaves or muffins won't turn out easily, let them stand for a minute or two, then run a knife around the sides and either invert or ease out.*

BRAN-BANANA MUFFINS

1 cup all-purpose flour
pinch of salt
1 teaspoon ground cinnamon
1 teaspoon apple pie spice
1 tablespoon baking powder
1⅓ cups coarsely crushed bran flakes
⅓ cup sugar
¼ cup butter, softened
3 large, ripe bananas
1 egg
½ cup milk
1½ tablespoons honey
few drops vanilla extract
¼ cup toasted sunflower seeds
or
¼ cup chopped pecans

Sift flour, salt, spices and baking powder. Mix in cereal and sugar. Cut in butter. Mash bananas and beat together with egg, milk, honey and vanilla. Add to flour mixture together with sunflower seeds or nuts. Mix lightly until just combined and spoon into greased muffin tins, filling them two-thirds full.

Bake at 400°F for 20 minutes. Let stand for a few minutes before removing from pan.
Makes 14

OVERNIGHT MUFFINS

1 cup whole-wheat flour
1 cup white bread flour or all-purpose flour
½ cup sugar
¼ cup vegetable oil
few drops vanilla extract
1½ teaspoons baking soda
1 egg, beaten
¼ teaspoon salt
1 cup milk
1 teaspoon ground cinnamon
¼ teaspoon grated nutmeg
¾ cup seedless raisins
¼ cup chopped walnuts or pecans (optional)

Mix all the ingredients, except raisins and nuts. Mix these in last. Cover batter and refrigerate overnight.

To bake, spoon into greased muffin pans, filling them three-quarters full.

Bake at 400°F for 15 to 20 minutes, until well risen and browned.
Makes about 18

HONEY-FRUIT MUFFINS

1 cup all-purpose flour
½ teaspoon salt
1 teaspoon baking soda
½ teaspoon apple pie spice
4 tablespoons soft light brown sugar
1 cup whole-wheat flour
¾ cup seedless raisins
3 tablespoons chopped mixed peel
1 egg
1 cup vegetable oil
4 tablespoons honey
1 cup buttermilk

Sift white flour, salt, baking soda and spice. Mix in sugar, whole-wheat flour, raisins and mixed peel. Beat together egg, oil, honey and buttermilk. Add to dry ingredients. Spoon into a greased muffin pan, filling three-quarters full.

Bake at 400°F for 20 to 22 minutes. Let stand for a minute, run a knife around the edges and remove.
Makes 12 muffins

GINGER-NUT MUFFINS

2 cups all-purpose flour
1 tablespoon baking powder
¼ teaspoon salt
2 teaspoons ground ginger
3 tablespoons sugar
4 knobs preserved ginger in syrup,
chopped
½ cup chopped walnuts or pecans
¼ cup vegetable oil
1 egg, beaten
½ cup milk
½ cup water
1½ tablespoons ginger syrup

Sift flour, baking powder, salt and ginger. Add sugar, chopped ginger and nuts. Beat oil, egg, milk, water and syrup together. Pour into a well in center of dry ingredients, mix quickly, using a wooden spoon. Spoon into a greased muffin pan, filling two-thirds full.

Bake at 400°F for 20 to 25 minutes. Cool slightly, then remove.
Makes 12

LIGHT CHOCOLATE MUFFINS

2 cups all-purpose flour
1 tablespoon baking powder
¼ teaspoon salt
1½ tablespoons cocoa powder
⅓ cup sugar
½ cup chopped walnuts or pecans
¼ cup vegetable oil
1 egg, beaten
½ cup milk
½ cup water
2 teaspoons instant coffee granules

Sift flour, baking powder, salt and cocoa. Add sugar and nuts. Beat oil, egg, milk, water and coffee granules together. Pour into a well in center of dry ingredients. Mix lightly, using a wooden spoon. Spoon into a greased muffin pan, two-thirds full.

Bake at 400°F for 20 to 25 minutes.
Makes 12

Savory muffins such as Cottage Cheese, Green Pepper and Onion Muffins, and Scallion, Cheese and Celery Muffins, go well with soup.

Carrot and Fruit Muffins; Health Muffins; Coconut-Currant Muffins.

CHEESE AND HERB MUFFINS

Great with soups or salads.

1 cup all-purpose flour
4 teaspoons baking powder
½ teaspoon salt
1 teaspoon dry mustard
1 cup whole-wheat flour
1 teaspoon Italian seasoning
2 teaspoons sugar
3 tablespoons finely chopped fresh parsley
¾ cup grated Cheddar cheese
1 egg
1 cup milk
¼ cup vegetable oil
extra grated cheese or sesame seeds

Sift flour, baking powder, salt and mustard. Mix in whole-wheat flour, herbs, sugar, parsley and cheese. Beat egg with milk and oil, pour into dry mixture and mix lightly. Spoon into greased muffin pans, filling them two-thirds full. Sprinkle with extra cheese or sesame seeds.

Bake at 400°F for 25 minutes. Cool slightly, then run a knife around the edges and remove. Serve with butter.
Makes 12 to 14

CARROT AND FRUIT MUFFINS

Add a handful of sunflower seeds or chopped walnuts for crunch.

2 tablespoons seedless raisins
3 tablespoons chopped mixed peel
1 cup water
¾–1 cup soft light brown sugar
¾ cup coarsely grated carrots
2 tablespoons butter
1 teaspoon apple pie spice
1 cup all-purpose flour
1 teaspoon baking soda
1 teaspoon baking powder
pinch of salt
1 cup whole-wheat flour
½ cup shredded coconut
few drops vanilla extract

Place fruit, water, sugar, carrots, butter and spice in saucepan. Bring to a boil, cover and simmer gently for 10 minutes. Leave to cool completely. Sift all-purpose flour, baking soda, baking powder and salt and stir into cooled mixture. Add whole-wheat flour, coconut and vanilla, and nuts, if using. Spoon into a greased muffin pan, filling two-thirds full. Bake at 400°F for 18 to 20 minutes. Let stand for 1 minute, then transfer to a wire rack.

Makes 12 to 14

> HINT
> ▪ *Whole-wheat and white flours can often be interchanged; however whole-wheat flour will need more liquid.*

HEALTH MUFFINS

These wholesome muffins, containing rye and whole-wheat flours, will not rise quite as high as those using refined ingredients. The molasses adds color and flavor, while the raisins and sunflower seeds provide extra nutrition.

½ cup self-rising flour
½ teaspoon salt
1½ teaspoons baking powder
1 teaspoon apple pie spice
6 tablespoons sugar
1 cup whole-wheat flour
½ cup rye flour
½ cup seedless raisins
¼ cup sunflower seeds
1 egg
1 cup buttermilk
4 teaspoons molasses
½ cup vegetable oil

Sift self-rising flour, salt, baking powder, spice and sugar. Mix in whole-wheat and rye flours. Add raisins and sunflower seeds. Beat together egg, buttermilk, molasses and oil. Add to flour mixture and mix lightly. Spoon into greased muffin pans, filling them two-thirds full. Bake at 400°F for 25 minutes. Cool on a wire rack.

Makes 16

NUTTY DATE MUFFINS

1½ cups finely chopped pitted dates
3 tablespoons chopped mixed peel
2 tablespoons butter
1 cup boiling water
½ cup all-purpose flour
1 teaspoon baking powder
1 teaspoon baking soda
pinch of salt
1 teaspoon ground cinnamon
¼ teaspoon grated nutmeg
pinch of ground cloves
1 cup whole-wheat flour
⅓ cup soft light brown sugar
⅓ cup chopped walnuts or pecans
few drops vanilla extract
7 tablespoons buttermilk

Put dates, mixed peel and butter into bowl. Pour boiling water over, stir to mix and then leave to cool. Sift all-purpose flour, baking powder, baking soda, salt and spices. Add whole-wheat flour and sugar. Mix in cooled date mixture, nuts and vanilla and then quickly moisten with buttermilk. Spoon into greased muffin pans, filling them two-thirds full. Bake at 400°F for 15 to 20 minutes. Cool on a wire rack.

Makes 12 to 16

COCONUT-CURRANT MUFFINS

2 cups all-purpose flour
1 tablespoon baking powder
¼ teaspoon salt
⅓ cup sugar
¾ cup shredded coconut
⅓ cup currants
¼ cup vegetable oil
1 egg, beaten
½ cup milk
½ cup water
extra shredded coconut

Sift flour, baking powder and salt. Add sugar, coconut and currants. Beat together the oil, egg, milk and water. Pour into well in center of dry ingredients. Mix lightly – the batter should be lumpy.

Spoon into a greased muffin pan, filling two-thirds full. Sprinkle top with extra shredded coconut.

Bake at 400°F for 20 to 25 minutes. Cool slightly, then transfer to a wire rack.

Makes 12

CHEESE MUFFINS

Using half milk and half water makes muffins especially light, as in these golden-brown savory muffins – delicious served hot with butter. For added flavor, strip the leaves off a few sprigs of fresh thyme and add with the cheese.

1½ cups all-purpose flour
1 tablespoon baking powder
¼ teaspoon salt
1 teaspoon dry mustard
¾ cup finely grated, sharp Cheddar cheese
1 teaspoon sugar
⅓ cup milk
⅓ cup water
¼ cup vegetable oil
1 egg
paprika and/or tiny cubes of cheese

Sift flour, baking powder, salt and mustard. Mix in cheese and sugar. Beat together milk, water, oil and egg. Add to flour mixture and stir quickly until just combined – mixture will not be smooth. Spoon into a greased muffin pan, filling two-thirds full. Sprinkle with paprika, placing a tiny cube of cheese in the middle, if using.

Bake on middle shelf of oven at 400°F for 25 minutes. Let stand for a minute, then run a knife around the edges to loosen, and remove.

Makes 12

BISCUITS

BASIC FEATHERLIGHT BISCUITS

Biscuits to serve with jam and whipped cream.

2 cups all-purpose flour
4 teaspoons baking powder
pinch of salt
1½ tablespoons sugar
¼ cup butter, softened
3 tablespoons milk
3 tablespoons water
1 egg
½ teaspoon lemon juice

GLAZE
1 egg yolk beaten with 1 teaspoon water

Sift flour, baking powder and salt together. Add sugar, then cut in butter. Beat together milk, water, egg and lemon juice. Pour into a well in the center of the dry ingredients. Mix lightly with a fork to a soft dough, then pat out on a lightly floured board. Working quickly, either cut into squares, or cut into circles with a 2½-inch cutter. Place on a lightly greased or nonstick baking sheet. Glaze the biscuits with egg-wash.

Bake toward top of oven at 425°F for 12 minutes. Serve as soon as possible.
Makes 10

GOLDEN-TOPPED CHEESE BISCUITS

2 cups all-purpose flour or white bread flour
4 teaspoons baking powder
½ teaspoon dry mustard
¼ teaspoon salt
pinch of cayenne pepper
1 cup grated Cheddar cheese
3 tablespoons vegetable oil
1 egg
3 tablespoons milk
3 tablespoons water

Basic Featherlight Biscuits;
Spicy Raisin Biscuits (page 73).

TOPPING
1½ tablespoons butter, melted
⅓ cup grated Cheddar cheese
½ teaspoon vegetable extract

Sift together flour, baking powder, mustard, salt and cayenne. Add cheese. Beat together oil, egg, milk and water. Pour into a well in center of dry ingredients and mix lightly with a fork until dough holds together. Pat out ¾ inch thick on a lightly floured board. Cut into circles with 2½-inch biscuit cutter and place on a greased baking sheet.

Mash together ingredients for topping and place a teaspoonful on top of each biscuit. Bake toward top of oven at 425°F for 12 minutes. Serve hot with butter.
Makes 10 to 12

DROPPED CHEESE BISCUITS

Exceptionally light and quickly-made biscuits, requiring no cutting; delicious served hot with butter for a special breakfast.

2 cups all-purpose flour
1 tablespoon baking powder
1 teaspoon sugar
¼ teaspoon salt
1 teaspoon dry mustard
⅓ cup grated sharp Cheddar cheese
1 egg
½ cup milk
6 tablespoons water
3 tablespoons vegetable oil
paprika

Sift the flour, baking powder, sugar, salt and dry mustard. Add the cheese. Beat the egg, milk, water and oil together. Make a well in the center of the dry ingredients and pour in the liquid. Mix quickly to a soft dough, using a fork. Drop spoonfuls onto a greased baking sheet. Lightly dust the tops with paprika.

Bake toward the top of the oven at 425°F for 10 to 12 minutes.
Makes 12

SOUR CREAM, SAGE AND CHIVE BISCUITS

A delicious, savory biscuit. If fresh herbs are not available, 1 teaspoon Italian seasoning may be substituted.

2 cups self-rising flour
¼ teaspoon salt
2 teaspoons sugar
½ cup sour cream
1½ tablespoons finely chopped fresh chives
16 fresh sage leaves, finely chopped
3 tablespoons finely chopped fresh parsley
1 egg
3 tablespoons water
milk and poppy seeds

Sift flour, salt and sugar. Mix in sour cream and herbs. Beat egg with water and add, mixing to a soft dough. Turn out onto a floured board and pat out ¾ inch thick. Cut into squares, or into circles, using a floured 2½-inch biscuit cutter and being careful not to twist when cutting. Place on a greased baking sheet. Brush with milk and sprinkle with poppy seeds. Bake toward top of oven at 425°F for 12 minutes. Serve hot.
Makes 8 to 10

LOW-FAT BISCUITS

Made without eggs or butter.

2 cups self-rising flour
¼ teaspoon salt
4 teaspoons sugar
3 tablespoons nonfat milk powder
⅔ cup water
¼ cup vegetable oil

Sift flour, salt and sugar together. Mix milk powder into water and beat together with oil. Add to flour mixture and mix lightly. Pat out ¾ inch thick on a lightly floured board. Cut out, using a 2½-inch cutter. Place on a greased baking sheet.

Bake toward top of oven at 425°F for 12 minutes. Serve hot, with butter and cheese, or jam.
Makes 10

WHOLE-FRUIT BISCUITS

Hearty wedges of fruity goodness.

1 cup white bread flour
4 teaspoons baking powder
½ teaspoon salt
1½ cups whole-wheat flour
⅔ cup mixed dried fruit
1½ tablespoons soft light brown sugar
1 teaspoon finely grated orange peel (optional)
1 egg
⅓ cup milk
⅓ cup water
5 tablespoons honey
⅓ cup vegetable oil

TOPPING
2 teaspoons sugar
½ teaspoon ground cinnamon

Sift the white bread flour, baking powder and salt together. Add whole-wheat flour, fruit, sugar and peel. Beat egg, milk, water, honey and oil together and pour into a well in center of dry ingredients. Using a fork, mix quickly to a soft dough. Pat out into a round on a lightly floured board. Brush with egg glaze or milk and sprinkle with topping. Using a sharp knife, cut into 8 to 10 wedges and place on a greased baking sheet.

Bake just above center of oven at 425°F for 15 to 18 minutes
Makes 8 to 10 wedges

GINGER BISCUITS

2 cups all-purpose flour
4 teaspoons baking powder
¼ teaspoon salt
1½ tablespoons sugar
1 teaspoon ground ginger
¼ cup butter
3–4 large knobs preserved ginger in syrup, finely chopped
3 tablespoons finely chopped mixed peel
¼ cup milk
¼ water
1 egg

Sift dry ingredients. Cut in butter. Add chopped ginger and mixed peel. Beat together milk, water and egg. Add to dry ingredients and mix lightly with a fork to a soft ball. Pat out ¾ inch thick on a floured board – you may have to flour your hands a little – and cut into 2½-inch rounds, squares, or triangles. Place on a greased baking sheet.

Bake toward top of oven at 425°F for 12 minutes.
Makes about 12

> NOTE
> ● *A dash of lemon juice added to the liquid will lighten scones and biscuits. When using a biscuit cutter, be careful not to twist when you cut out the dough.*

PUMPKIN BISCUITS

Serve these biscuits with butter and honey. Use a bright orange, firm-fleshed pumpkin, and drain well after cooking.

¼ cup butter, softened
½ cup soft light brown sugar
1 egg, lightly beaten
3 cups self-rising flour
½ teaspoon salt
2 teaspoons ground ginger
1 teaspoon ground cinnamon
pinch of ground cloves
½ cup seedless raisins
1 cup smooth pumpkin purée
3 tablespoons chopped mixed peel

Cream butter and sugar. Beat in egg, adding 1 teaspoon of the flour. Sift flour, salt and spices and add. Mix well. Add raisins, pumpkin and mixed peel. Mix to a soft dough – no liquid is required, as the purée should moisten the mixture sufficiently. Pat out ¾ inch thick onto a floured board and cut into circles, using a floured 2½-inch biscuit cutter. Place on a greased baking sheet and brush tops with egg glaze. Bake just above center of oven at 425°F for 12 minutes.
Makes 14 to 16

WHOLE-WHEAT CHEESE BISCUITS

1 cup white bread flour
1 tablespoon baking powder
¼ teaspoon salt
2 teaspoons sugar
1 teaspoon dry mustard
1 cup whole-wheat flour
3 tablespoons butter
1 cup grated Cheddar cheese
1 egg
3 tablespoons milk
3 tablespoons water

GLAZE
1 egg yolk beaten with 1 teaspoon water
paprika

Sift white flour, baking powder, salt, sugar and mustard. Add whole-wheat flour. Cut in butter, then add cheese. Beat egg, milk and water together and add. Mix with a fork and then lightly form into a ball, adding, if necessary, 1–2 teaspoons water. Pat out on a lightly floured board and cut into nine squares. Place on a greased baking sheet. Brush with egg wash and sprinkle lightly with paprika.

Bake toward top of oven at 425°F for 12 minutes. Serve hot with butter and honey.
Makes 9

SPICY FRUIT BISCUITS

2 cups self-rising flour
¼ teaspoon salt
1 teaspoon apple pie spice
1½ tablespoons sugar
¼ cup butter, softened
½ cup mixed dried fruit
1 egg
3 tablespoons milk
3 tablespoons water

TOPPING
milk
1 teaspoon sugar
½ teaspoon ground cinnamon

Sift flour, salt and spice. Add sugar and cut in butter. Add dried fruit. Beat egg, milk and water. Pour into a well in center of dry ingredients and mix lightly with a fork. When thoroughly combined, pat out on a lightly floured board. Cut into squares or circles, using a 2½-inch biscuit cutter. Place on a greased baking sheet. Brush with milk and sprinkle with sugar mixed with cinnamon. Bake just above center of oven at 425°F for 12 minutes.
Makes 10

NOTE
● *Instead of breaking an egg just for glazing, milk may be substituted. The resulting biscuit, however, will not have the same rich brown color.*

JIFFY BISCUITS

Light, white biscuits that rise like little stuffed pillows, especially if cut into squares instead of circles. Remember that cutters, if twisted, will frighten the life out of biscuits. These biscuits may be served with either sweet or savory accompaniments.

2 cups self-rising flour
¼ teaspoon salt
1 tablespoon sugar
1 egg
¼ cup vegetable oil
buttermilk
milk or egg-wash

Sift the flour, salt and sugar together. Break the egg into a measuring cup. Add the oil and enough buttermilk to fill the cup to the 7-ounce mark. Beat well, then add to dry ingredients. Mix quickly, using a fork, until mixture holds together, then toss into a ball with your hands. Pat out ¾ inch thick on a lightly floured board, then cut into desired shapes. Place on a greased baking sheet and brush with milk or egg-wash.

Bake just above center of oven at 425°F for 12 minutes.
Makes about 10

Golden-topped Cheese Biscuits; Jiffy Biscuits; Sour Cream, Sage and Chive Biscuits.

SPICY RAISIN BISCUITS

1 cup all-purpose flour
4 teaspoons baking powder
3 tablespoons sugar
1 teaspoon apple pie spice
½ teaspoon salt
1 cup whole-wheat flour
1 cup seedless raisins
1 egg
¼ cup milk
¼ cup water
¼ cup vegetable oil

TOPPING
milk
1 teaspoon sugar
1 teaspoon ground cardamom or cinnamon

Sift all-purpose flour, baking powder, sugar, spice and salt together. Add the whole-wheat flour and raisins and toss until coated. Beat the egg, milk, water and oil together. Pour all at once into a well in the center of the dry ingredients and, using a fork, mix to a soft dough. As soon as the mixture holds together, turn out onto a lightly floured board. Pat the dough out until ¾ inch thick. The dough will be soft, therefore you should flour a 2½-inch biscuit cutter before cutting out circles. Arrange the biscuits on a greased baking sheet and brush the tops with milk and sprinkle with sugar and spice.

Bake just above the center of the oven at 425°F for 12 minutes.
Makes 12

YEAST BREADS

Bread-baking is a long and involved story, dating right back to the Stone Age, when grain was crushed between two stones, mixed to a dough with water, shaped into thin cakes and baked on a stone over a fire. As can be imagined, these bread cakes were hard and very chewy. The triumph of discovering "risen" bread is ascribed to a forgetful Egyptian, who mixed some dough and then went off somewhere on his camel, leaving the dough sitting in the hot sun – whereupon it fermented, and rose. Another, more plausible story, is that they learned to use the yeasty foam from the top of their fermenting wines.

In due course, the Egyptians grew so much wheat that they were able to export it. The Greeks bought much of the grain, and were so quick to develop the art of baking beautiful breads that they became the master bakers of the period. The skill was further developed by the conquering Romans, who eventually introduced their knowledge to Britain. It is said that Cassius was so appalled by the quality of the bread he found on his arrival in Britain, that he immediately signaled his baker in Rome to send him some that he could eat.

It took many centuries before proper mills were developed and bread became a commodity within everyone's reach. Today, of course, due to mechanization, bread in all its forms is available everywhere.

Basically, bread is made from flour, yeast, salt and liquid, and kneading it allows the gluten in the flour to stretch and form an elastic framework around the gas bubbles from the yeast.

Flour: There are three main types of wheat flour widely available for bread-baking. White bread, or hard, flour is used for most white breads. It has a high gluten content, and produces loaves of a creamy color. All-purpose white flour is highly refined and produces finely textured, fluffy rolls; it may also be used for breads.

Whole-wheat flour has a high percentage of bran and wheat germ. Bread made from this flour is dark in color, has a slightly nutty flavor and a dense coarse texture.

Flours made from other grains, like rye, have very little gluten and should always be mixed with a wheat flour. Soybean flour is rich in protein, and helps bread to remain fresh and moist.

As far as rising times and the amount of water absorbed are concerned, please be prepared to adapt; there are few hard and fast rules, and it really is a matter of trial and perception. Sometimes a dough will "draw" together quickly into a ball – at other times you could add the same amount of water and find it looks flaky. Different flours vary as to absorption capacity, and this must always be borne in mind. Nevertheless, yeast baking should be tackled with confidence and enthusiasm. Short of not activating the yeast by using water that is too cool, or killing it with water that is too hot, if yeast is properly kneaded it will eventually spring up. Yeast is tougher than most people think; the water should be warm rather than cold.

Yeast: Yeast is a living substance composed of tiny cells. When provided with moisture, food and warmth, the cells grow and give off carbon dioxide. It is this gas which causes the dough to rise. Yeast also gives off alcohol, which is driven off by the heat of the oven, but which can give the bread a sour taste if the dough is left to rise for too long. And, please, do not think that by using more yeast you will get a better rise – the bread will simply taste yeasty. Yeast should not be hurried and, given time, even relatively small quantities will rise heavy doughs.

For the sake of convenience, I have used active dry yeast in all recipes requiring yeast. It is available in envelopes, and, unlike fresh compressed yeast, it keeps well – although once opened, it is best to store it, sealed, in the refrigerator. Rapid-rise dry yeast is sold in envelopes and has a long shelf life, but should also be used right away once opened.

When dissolving active dry yeast, the water temperature is most important. If it is too hot, the yeast cells will be killed; if too cold, they will not grow. A little warmer than lukewarm is about right, but experience remains the best teacher.

A little sugar is usually added to the water as food for the yeast, and the yeast is then sprinkled onto the sugar-water's surface. Do not stir, but leave the yeast to froth, and then give it a quick stir to make sure that all the granules have dissolved just before adding it to the flour.

Liquid: Water is, naturally, the easiest liquid to use and provides the best volume and will result in a thick, crisp crust. The addition of milk, however, will make the bread more nutritious and it also improves the texture of the crumb and results in a softer crust.

I always scald the milk first, and then leave it to cool to lukewarm – scalding destroys any bacteria and makes the dough somewhat easier to handle. The amount of liquid added to a dough varies, depending on the type of flour used. Start with the specified amount, and if the dough appears flaky, make more small additions until the required elasticity is reached. Once kneaded, further liquid cannot be successfully added to a dough, although extra flour can be incorporated into a too-soft dough.

Salt: Bread without salt is not palatable, but salt should be used with discretion. It prevents the yeast from fermenting too quickly, thereby providing a good texture due to a slower rising, but too much salt will kill the yeast and then the dough won't rise at all. Too little salt results in a coarse crumb.

Sugar: Apart from being a food for the yeast, sugar also gives color to bread's crust. Because sugar slows down the fermentation process, sweet yeast loaves require a longer rising period than plain breads. Remember that too much sugar will produce a poorly risen loaf.

Fat: Butter, margarine or lard are regarded as the best shortenings for improving a bread's keeping qualities, increasing volume, and adding to the flavor and softness of crumb. Oil may also be used, especially in the baking of "health" breads, but it does nothing for the color of the loaf.

Eggs: These are sometimes added to enrich and color bread. Breads containing eggs also have a tender crust.

Dried fruit, cheese, vegetables: The addition of these makes the dough heavier and results in a longer rising period.

Kneading: Turn out the dough onto a lightly floured board and be prepared for a 10 minute session. I do not think one can ever overknead a dough, and underkneading will have an undesirable result – so roll up your sleeves and punch away. The idea is to fold the dough over and then push it down and away from you with the heels of your palms; turn it slightly – I find a counter-clockwise movement comes most naturally – and then fold and press down again. On and on. It becomes quite hypnotic eventually, especially when the dough starts responding by becoming smooth and soft and pliable, without being sticky.

If the dough feels too sticky, sprinkle a little extra flour on the board and carry on – if necessary sprinkle on more flour, but do so a little at a time so that you don't make the dough too stiff, in which case it cannot "balloon."

Rising: To avoid a crust forming on top of the dough, brush the mixing bowl with oil, turn the dough in it to coat the top, then cover with a dish towel.

Another method is to cover the bowl with a damp towel. The dough is then left to rise in a warm, draft-free place.

Rising times vary, depending on the temperature in your kitchen – in cold weather it will, of course, take longer. Rising times are also affected by the amount of yeast, the kind of flour, and the extra ingredients used.

I like to put the bowl in the warming drawer of my oven. I turn it on briefly beforehand and then turn it off again. If the dough is allowed to get too hot, the bread will be coarse and will break. As a general rule, the dough should double in volume. If allowed to over-rise, however, the loaf will have a coarse texture and poor flavor, while under-rising produces a heavy loaf with a loose top.

Second rising: Once doubled, punch down the dough by pushing your fist into the middle, turn it inward and over, and knead again for a minute or two to break up the pockets of gas. For really fine-textured bread, it may be left to rise again – but this is time-consuming. Alternatively, either shape the dough immediately, or better still, cover it and let it rest for 10 minutes, and then shape and cover.

Greased plastic wrap is convenient because it does not lie heavily on the dough. Do not cover tightly – leave space for air to circulate. Leave to rise until doubled in volume, or nearly doubled in some cases, in a warm spot.

Glazing: Breads and rolls are usually glazed just before baking and, although egg-wash is often recommended, especially when baking rolls, I usually use milk – breaking an egg just for glazing seems an unnecessary extravagance, and milk or water or a sugar-water solution are satisfactory. Coarsely cracked wheat, and sesame, sunflower and poppy seeds, all make attractive finishes. With certain breads or rolls a pan of boiling water may be placed on the bottom shelf of the oven to encourage a shiny, crisp crust.

Baking: Even with sweet breads, which are usually baked at lower temperatures than other breads, I like to start them off with a hot oven to stop the fermentation of the yeast. Exact temperatures and positioning in the oven are specified

with each recipe – it is important to abide by them to avoid overbrowning.

To test whether a loaf (or a roll) is baked, turn it over and knock on the bottom – it should sound distinctly hollow. If in doubt, return to the oven, out of the pan and upside down, for a short while at a lower temperature. Always cool bread completely on a wire rack before storing.

Mishaps: Here again experience is the best teacher and the more you bake with yeast, the sooner you will learn the reason for imperfect results and how to avoid them. However, a few pointers may help. The greatest mistakes are in making a dough too wet or too dry, under- or over-rising, and insufficient kneading. These will result in loaves that have poor volume, an uneven shape, heavy texture, holes and a coarse crumb, with a crust that either breaks at the sides, or is very thick and has a poor crumb color. Over-risen dough, especially in too warm a place, also results in a strong yeast taste.

Using a pan of the wrong size also spells disaster to the shape of a loaf – if the pan is too small, you'll end up with an irregular shape and a cracked crust. Frankly, there's such a long list of possible faults that it is best just to follow the recipes carefully, remembering the main points I have listed, and the importance of the correct temperature – in dissolving the yeast, during rising and in baking.

Shaping breads: The traditional pan-shaped loaf has great appeal. Press the dough into a rectangle and then fold inward from each side. Drop into the pan with the seam underneath. A farm-house-style loaf may be made by slashing the top lengthwise, creating a sunburst effect. Braids are also most effective – divide the dough into three pieces, roll into sausage shapes and braid – but not too tightly. Cobs are made by shaping the dough into a round ball, then flattening it slightly before placing on a floured baking sheet, leaving to rise and then sprinkling the top with flour before baking. Cottage loaves are made in the same way as cottage rolls, but are larger. A bloomer loaf is a long loaf with blunt ends and a flat top, fatter than French bread, and slashed on top before leaving to rise. While rising, these loaves, which are not placed in pans, should be supported on the sides with crumpled dish towels so they do not spread sideways too much. Pans other than traditional bread pans may be used, such as ring molds, or round cake pans, as in crown loaves. These are among the most attractive of breads: the dough is shaped into rolls, and arranged around the circumference of the pan, with one roll in the middle. They are then topped with grated cheese or sesame or poppy seeds. During rising and baking, these rolls join to form a "crown" of humped buns.

SWEET YEAST BREADS

Although these are not as straightforward as ordinary breads, the different shapes and decorations are fun to make. I have included a few recipes, mostly of European origin, where they are most popular. Due to the addition of "heavy" ingredients they will take longer to rise and prove, and although they are usually baked at a lower temperature because they brown more quickly, I like to start them off at a high temperature, as I said, to kill the yeast, and then reduce the temperature after about 10 minutes. They are usually baked toward the top of the oven. Sweet yeast breads may either be decorated before baking, or left to cool, and simply frosted. They go stale quite quickly, and may then be toasted.

ROLLS

Rolls are baked at a high temperature toward the top of the oven, and best if eaten fresh. Experiment with different shapes – round rolls; sausage-shaped finger rolls; snails, twists and knots, which are made by rolling the dough into long thin sausage shapes; cottage rolls, in which a small ball of dough is placed on top of a larger round and secured by pushing your finger through the center; and crescents, which, like croissants, are shaped by rolling a trian-gle up from the long end and easing into a horseshoe shape.

RUSKS

I have included kneaded rusks and "easy" rusks among the recipes for rolls – good for dunking. It is important, when separating rusks, not to slice them as this does affect the flavor. It is fine to use a knife as an aid, but it is better to use the tines of a fork. Whatever you do, always try to break them through, and dry them out on baking sheets in a very low oven so they end up crisped without browning.

QUICK BREADS

Whether sweet or savory, these are great time-savers and require no rising times as they are made with self-rising flour, baking powder, or baking soda and cream of tartar. Cheese and/or nuts are often used in these loaves, and it is useful to have a ready grated or chopped supply available. I grate large quantities of cheese in my food processor, using the grinding blade, and then store it in plastic bags in my freezer. The same applies to nuts, but be careful not to grind them too finely, otherwise the end product will not have the same texture. Sweet quick breads are often more flavorful if left for a day or two before slicing.

BISCUITS

It goes without saying that biscuits should always be eaten fresh. They are baked at a high temperature, toward the top of the oven. It is preferable not to roll them out before cutting – patting is better – to ensure lightness, and if using a cutter, be sure not to twist it as you cut. If you do, the biscuits will not rise as they should. A dash of lemon juice will also help to lighten biscuits.

MUFFINS

The golden rule here is never to overmix; muffin batter will usually be lumpy rather than smooth. Never over-fill the pan because the muffins will rise over the sides and be difficult to remove. As with rusks, break, rather than slice them in half before buttering.

COOKIES

I have tried to keep the time expended in cookie-making to a minimum because few of us, these days, can indulge in rolling and cutting and baking sheet after sheet of cookies as they used to do in Grandma's time. So I have included many recipes for cookies that are simply rolled into balls. There are also some refrigerator cookies, which only need to be sliced once they are chilled, and bar cookies, which are especially convenient when it comes to speed – but do try to use the size of pan recommended so the cookies are neither too thick nor too thin.

Using soft (not melted) butter when creaming a cookie dough makes the job much easier and ensures successful results. Insufficient creaming can result in a mixture that is too dry to shape, so here the electric mixer comes in handy.

Fat: I have included several recipes using oil instead of butter to cope with differing tastes and budgets. This will also make them more suitable for low-cholesterol diets. These cookies are sometimes more difficult to handle, but are well worth attempting, and are often the crispest and most economical.

I also find oil best for greasing pans and baking sheets for all baking. Whenever possible, and especially in the case of cookies rich in butter, position the baking sheets on the middle shelf of the oven, to avoid overbrowning on the bottom; if time allows, it is therefore better to bake cookies in relays.

Certain nutritious and unrefined ingredients have been introduced in several of the recipes, because it has been my experience that these are becoming increasingly popular, especially with teenagers.

Storing: Once cooled on wire racks, cookies should be stored in airtight containers. It is a good idea, in the case of crisp biscuits, to sprinkle each layer with a little sugar to keep them crunchy.

INDEX

A
Almond
  crescents 19
  meringue fingers 30
Aniseed milk rusks 53
Apple raisin and honey muffins 65

B
Baker's pride bread 39
Baking powder bread 55
Baking powder cob, plain 56
Baking powder rolls 50
Banana loaf 63
Batter bread *see also* Health
    Breads, Quick Breads *and*
    Yeast Breads
  cheese, onion and garlic 46
  enriched 44
  four seed 46
  nutty whole-wheat 47
  oatmeal, with herbs 47
  whole-wheat, instant 46
Beer bread 55
Biscuits
  dropped cheese 71
  featherlight, basic 71
  fruit, spicy 72
  ginger 72
  golden-topped cheese 71
  jiffy 73
  low-fat 71
  pumpkin 72
  raisin, spicy 73
  sour cream, sage and chive 71
  whole-wheat cheese 72
  whole-wheat fruit 72
Bran
  banana muffins 66
  flake-buttermilk rusks 53
  flake crisps 15
  fruit loaf 59
Brown herb bread braid 43
Brown sugar cookies 18
Brownies 9
Butter cookies, basic 10
Buttermilk
  fruit loaf 63
  rusks 53
  scone bread 56
  whole-wheat soda bread with rosemary 44

C
Caramel squares 29
Caraway rye loaf 46
Carrot
  and coconut jumbles 12
  and fruit muffins 68

date and sunflower seed
    cookies 25
Cheese
  biscuits, dropped 71
  biscuits, golden-topped 71
  biscuits, whole-wheat 72
  and caraway cottage loaf 40
  and herb muffins 68
  crescents, quick 51
  feta, and garlic rolls 51
  muffins 69
  onion and garlic batter bread 46
  onion and nut bread 56
  soda bread, savory 55
Cheese-topped onion crown loaf 40
Chinese chews 25
Chocolate
  carrot and ginger loaf 60
  chip cookies 22
  cookies 11
  crinkles 20
  croissants 50
  digestives 27
  logs 21
  meringues 33
  muffins, light 67
  oatmeal refrigerator squares 31
  squares, frosted 29
  swirls, featherlight 29
Cinnamon-jam cookies 16
Clove-studded spicy brown cookies 29
Cocoa crisps, simple 24
Coconut
  almond crisps 13
  cherry stars 19
  currant muffins 69
  currant snaps 12
  lemon crispies 10
  macaroons 19
  shortbread fingers 34
  slices 15
  yogurt loaf 60
Coffee-glazed nutmeg loaf 55
Cookies and bars
  almond crescents 19
  almond meringue fingers 30
  bran flake crisps 15
  brown sugar cookies 18
  brownies 9
  butter, basic 10
  butter, coffee-pecan 10
  butter, lemon-peel 10
  caramel squares 29
  carrot and coconut jumbles 12
  carrot, date and sunflower seed 25

Chinese chews 25
chocolate 11
chocolate chip 22
chocolate crinkles 20
chocolate digestives 27
chocolate logs 21
chocolate-oatmeal refrigerator squares 31
chocolate squares, frosted 29
chocolate swirls, featherlight 29
cinnamon-jam cookies 16
clove-studded spicy brown 29
cocoa crisps, simple 24
coconut-almond crisps 13
coconut-cherry stars 19
coconut-currant snaps 12
coconut-lemon crispies 10
coconut macaroons 19
coconut slices 15
cookie-press cookies 10
crunchies 21
date-and-nut bars, quick 25
date knobs 11
date, nut and oatmeal 30
Easter cookies 15
Florentines 12
fruit bars, quick 31
fruit drops 30
fruit-oatmeal squares 22
fruit squares, five-star 30
fruity refrigerator squares 16
fruity oatmeal crisps 20
gingerbread men 32
granny's gingersnaps 16
honeyed seed cookies 26
jam squares, old-fashioned 18
lemon sesame snaps 9
lemon-golden raisin snaps 22
melting moments 12
meringues 33
mocha-chocolate logs 16
muesli bars 19
muesli munchies 25
munchies 10
nut and oatmeal cookies 9
oatmeal and coconut 30
oatmeal, golden raisin and coconut bars 24
orange and oatmeal macaroons 26
orange cookie-press cookies 22
orange liqueur wafers 25
orange, honey and raisin crisps 26
party faces 33
peanut butter cookies 20
raisin-and-bran bars, one-bowl 14

raisin-oatmeal bars 20
snickerdoodles 16
sour cream-spice 14
spice cookies 9
spiced coconut cookies 21
spiced coffee drops 19
spiced mincemeat bars 26
spiced pecan crisps 15
spiced golden raisin slices 15
sunflower seed and honey cookies 26
vanilla condensed milk drops 13
vanilla Viennese twirls 21
walnut crisps 24
wheat germ and muesli crisps 14
whole-wheat-and-oatmeal ginger crisps 22
whole-wheat, honey and coconut crisps 12
Corn bread 55
Croissants 50
  Chocolate 50
  whole-wheat 50
Crunchies 21

D
Date
  and nut bars, quick 25
  knobs 11
  loaf 58
  nut and oatmeal cookies 30
Dropped cheese biscuits 71

E
Easter cookies 15
Enriched batter bread 44

F
Featherlight biscuits, basic 71
Feta cheese and garlic rolls 51
Florentines 12
Four seed batter bread 46
French bread 38
Frosted chocolate squares 29
Fruit
  bars, quick 31
  biscuits, spicy 72
  biscuits, whole-wheat 72
  and carrot loaf 58
  drops 30
  loaf, brown 57
  muffins, favorite 65
  oatmeal squares 22
  squares, five-star 30
  tea loaf 60
Fruity refrigerator squares 16
Fruity oatmeal crisps 20

G

Ginger
  biscuits 72
  nut muffins 67
Ginger-glazed shortbread 34
Gingerbread
  men 32
  nutty dark 58
Golden-topped cheese biscuits
  71
Granny's gingersnaps 16
Green pepper and onion
  muffins 66

H

Health breads *see also* Batter
  Breads, Quick Breads *and*
  Yeast Breads
  batter, enriched 44
  brown herb bread braid 43
  buttermilk whole-wheat soda,
    with rosemary 44
  caraway rye loaf 46
  cheese, onion and garlic
    batter 46
  four-seed batter 46
  nutty brown bloomer loaf 43
  nutty whole-wheat batter 47
  oatmeal batter, with herbs 47
  pumpernickel 45
  whole-wheat batons with
    garlic and fresh herbs 43
  whole-wheat batter, instant 46
  whole-wheat honey 44
  whole-wheat nut, raisin and
    yogurt 44
Health muffins 69
Herb
  bread braid, brown 43
  bread braid, white 37
  bread, buttermilk 55
  bread, Italian 39
  muffins, processor 65
Honey-fruit muffins 66
Honeyed seed cookies 26

I

Irish soda bread 56
Italian herb bread 39

J

Jam squares, old-fashioned 18
Jiffy biscuits 73

L

Lemon
  loaf, glazed 60
  sesame snaps 9
  golden raisin snaps 22
Light chocolate muffins 67
Low-fat biscuits 71

M

Melt-away shortbread 35
Melting moments 12
Meringues 33
  almond meringue fingers 30
Mocha
  chocolate logs 16
  pecan shortbread 35

Muesli
  bars 19
  munchies 25
Muffin pan whole-wheat rolls 50
Muffins
  apple, raisin and honey 65
  basic 65
  bran-banana 66
  carrot and fruit 68
  cheese 69
  cheese and herb 68
  chocolate, light 67
  coconut-currant 69
  fruit, favorite 65
  ginger-nut 67
  green pepper and onion 66
  health 69
  herb, processor 65
  honey-fruit 66
  nutty date 69
  overnight 66
  scallion, cheese and celery 66
Munchies 10

N

Nut and oatmeal cookies 9
Nutty brown bloomer loaf 43
Nutty dark gingerbread 58
Nutty date muffins 69
Nutty whole-wheat batter
  bread 47

O

Oatmeal
  and coconut cookies 30
  batter bread with herbs 47
  golden raisins and coconut
    bars 24
Old-fashioned jam squares 18
One-bowl
  orange loaf 62
  raisin and bran bars 14
Orange
  and oatmeal macaroons 26
  cookie-press cookies 22
  honey and raisin crisps 26
  liqueur wafers 25
  loaf, one-bowl 62
Overnight muffins 66

P

Party faces 33
Peanut butter cookies 20
Pita breads 52
  whole-wheat 52
Poppy seed braid 38
Pumpernickel bread 45
Pumpkin
  pecan and raisin loaf 63
  biscuits 72

Q

Quick breads *see also* Batter
  Breads, Health Breads *and*
  Yeast Breads
  baking powder 55
  baking powder cob, plain 56
  banana loaf 63
  beer 55
  bran-fruit loaf 59

buttermilk-fruit loaf 63
buttermilk-herb 55
buttermilk biscuits 56
cheese soda, savory 55
cheese, onion and nut 56
chocolate, carrot and ginger
  loaf 60
coconut-yogurt loaf 60
coffee-glazed nutmeg loaf 58
corn 55
date loaf 58
fruit and carrot loaf 58
fruit loaf, brown 57
fruit tea loaf 60
Irish soda 56
lemon loaf, glazed 60
nutty dark gingerbread 58
one-bowl orange loaf 62
pumpkin, pecan and raisin
  loaf 63
spiced honey loaf 59
surprise loaf 63
zucchini bread 57

R

Raisin
  biscuits, spicy 73
  and bran bars, one-bowl 14
  oatmeal bars 20
Rolls
  baking powder 50
  feta cheese and garlic 51
  muffin pan whole-wheat 50
  rosemary 49
  white 49
Rusks
  aniseed milk 53
  bran flake-buttermilk 53
  buttermilk 53
  slab 53
  whole-wheat 52, 53

S

Savory cheese soda bread 55
Scallion, cheese and celery
  muffins 66
Scots shortbread, rich 34
Shortbread
  coconut fingers 34
  ginger-glazed 34
  melt-away 35
  mocha-pecan 35
  pennies 34
  Scots, rich 34
  spicy 35
Slab rusks 53
Snickerdoodles 16
Soda bread
  buttermilk whole-wheat with
    rosemary 44
  cheese, savory 55
  Irish 56
Sour cream
  sage and chive scones 71
  spice cookies 14
Spice cookies 9
Spiced
  coconut cookies 21
  coffee drops 19
  fruit braid 40

golden raisin slices 15
honey loaf 59
mincemeat bars 26
pecan crisps 15
Spicy
  fruit biscuits 72
  raisin biscuits 73
  shortbread 35
Sunflower seed and honey
  cookies 26
Surprise loaf 63
Swedish tea ring 41

V

Vanilla
  condensed milk drops 13
  Viennese twirls 21

W

Walnut crisps 24
Wheat germ and muesli crisps
  14
White bread, basic 37
White farmhouse bread 37
White herb bread braid 37
White ring bread 38
White rolls 49
Whole-wheat
  and oatmeal-ginger crisps 22
  batons with garlic and fresh
    herbs 43
  batter bread, instant 46
  cheese biscuits 72
  croissants 50
  fruit biscuits 72
  honey and coconut crisps 14
  honey bread 44
  nut, raisin and yogurt bread
    44
  pitas 52
  rolls, muffin pan 50
  rusks 52, 53

Y

Yeast breads
  baker's pride 39
  cheese and caraway cottage
    loaf 40
  cheese, onion and garlic
    batter 46
  cheese-topped onion crown
    loaf 40
  French 38
  Italian herb 39
  poppy seed braid 38
  spiced fruit braid 40
  Swedish tea ring 41
  white farmhouse 37
  white herb bread braid
  white ring 38
  white, basic 37

Z

Zucchini bread 57